IT IS MY SOUL THAT SINGS

SELECTED POEMS OF CHARLES GORDON REX

EDITED BY CHARLES GORDON REX, JR.

En Route Books and Media, LLC

St. Louis, MO

En Route Books and Media, LLC
5705 Rhodes Avenue
St. Louis, MO 63109

Cover credit: Photo of Charles Gordon Rex, provided by Charles Gordon Rex, Jr. Formatting by TJ Burdick.

Library of Congress Control Number: 2020952322

ISBN-13: 978-1-952464-40-9, 978-1-952464-46-1, 978-1-952464-56-0

Copyright © 2020 Charles Gordon Rex, Jr.
All rights reserved.

No part of this booklet may be reproduced, stored in a retrieval system, or transmitted in any form, or by any means, electronic, mechanical, photocopying, or otherwise, without the prior written permission of the author. Recitation is permitted.

DEDICATION

To Papa

TABLE OF CONTENTS

Biography of Charles Gordon Rex vii

1. Listen to My Song 3
2. Last Man, The 4
3. Prodigals, The 5
4. Child of Summer, A 6
5. Adventure 7
6. Ambition 8
7. And Thus It Is 9
8. And When I Come to Die 10
9. Anniversary 11
10. Another 12
11. Another Song 13
12. As Before 14
13. As One Who Walks 15

14. Autumn 16
15. Awakening, The 18
16. Autumnal Equinox 20
17. Bachelorhood 21
18. Bending Trees 22
19. Blow Gently 23
20. Books 24
21. The Bowery 26
22. Boy that He Was, The 27
23. Cathy Sue 28
24. Change 30
25. Chant For Spring 31
26. Christmas 32

27. Cinquains 33	46. First Born 55
28. Clouds At Sunset 34	47. First Love 56
29. Contentment 35	48. For Certain Talk 57
30. Conversation in the Rain, A 36	49. Four Books 58
31. Couplets – A Few Readings 38	50. Fragrance 60
32. Courage 40	51. Friends 61
33. Cricket, The 41	52. From Here To There 62
34. Dawn, The 42	53. From My New House 63
35. Dead, The 43	54. Fulfillment 64
36. Departure 44	55. Gambler, The 65
37. Destiny 45	56. Gemini 66
38. Dinner Party, The 46	57. Gifts 67
39. Disconsolate 47	58. Greater Fear, A 68
40. Door, The 48	59. Guest, The 70
41. Dreamers 49	60. Half A Journey 72
42. Dreams Of Youth 50	61. Half A Loaf 73
43. E Finito 51	62. Happy To His Arms 74
44. Fairwell To Unborn Fame 52	63. Happiness 76
45. Faint Heart, The 54	64. History 77

65. Human Nature 78

66. Hymn of Praise, A 79

67. I Can See The Sky 80

68. I Died A Year Ago Today 81

69. I Will Ask Only That 82

70. I Would Not Tarry More 83

71. If I Could Know 84

72. If Only 85

73. If You Speak 86

74. Imagery 87

75. Immortality 88

76. Implacable 89

77. In Search Of Truth 90

78. Imprisonment 92

79. Incognito 93

80. Jesus Of Nazareth 94

81. Laughter 96

82. The Last Bloom (A Sonnet Cycle) 97

83. Liberation 113

84. Last Day of June 114

85. Little Feet 116

86. A Lie Comes Quicker 118

87. Logic 119

88. Love 144

89. Loves We Knew, The 145

90. March and the Maiden 146

91. Musing in an Unknown Tongue 147

92. My Children's Mother 148

93. My Finest Thoughts 150

94. Nature's Plan 151

95. No Place For Me 152

96. No Talking Now 153

97. November 154

98. Of Beauty 155

99. Of Passion 156

100. Oh, Come, My Love 157

iii

101. Old Garden in Winter, An .. 158

102. On Moving To Florida 159

103. On Seeing a White Moth in Times Square 160

104. On Reading a Borrowed Book 162

105. Our Little Minds 163

106. Our Thoughts 164

107. Paradox 165

108. Park, A 166

109. Perspective 167

110. Poet Woos in Ancient Style, The 168

111. Potentiality 170

112. Presence 171

113. Prisoner 172

114. Profundity 173

115. Quest 174

116. Respite 175

117. Red-Breasted Grosbeak, The 176

118. Rose in the Book, The 178

119. Sea Moods 180

120. Sea, The 181

121. Seasons Flutter, The 182

122. Seeker, The 183

123. Silence 184

124. Snow Dances, The 185

125. Solitary 186

126. Sometime Perhaps Not Very Far Away 187

127. Song Of The Harvest 188

128. Sounds 189

129. Spring Thaw 190

130. Stray Thought, A 191

131. Strength 192

132. Sunrise 193

133. Teller of Tales, A 194

134. That You May Not Know 199

135. There Are Days 200

136. There Is A Church 201

137. There Was A Time 202

138. There Were Those Years 204

139. Things in Hand, The 205

140. This Strange Current 206

141. This Tiny Lake 207

142. Those Who Pass By 208

143. This Very Moment 210

144. Thought For Thought 211

145. Thoughts 212

146. Thrush's Song, The 213

147. 'Tis Evening 214

148. To Die 215

149. To My Wife 216

150. To Grow In Grace 218

151. To Sit In Judgment 219

152. Today I Live 220

153. Toil 221

154. Too Many 222

155. Transition 223

156. Tree, The 224

157. Trivialities 225

158. Truth 226

159. Vows 227

160. Warning 228

161. Waves 229

162. We Come Without A By-Your-Leave 230

163. What Is Past 231

164. What Lurks Behind Your Eyes 232

165. What Things She Loved 233

166. What You Have To Give 234

167. When Red Leaves Fall 235

168. Whippoorwill, The 236

169. Why Sadness 237

170. Wind Storm 238

171. Words 239

172. You Stand Before Me 240

173. Youthful Thought, A 243

174. Zenith 244

About the Editor 245

Charles Gordon Rex
June 20, 1909 – April 23, 1973
Biography

Charles Gordon Rex was born in Springfield, Massachusetts, on June 20, 1909, into a family of nine brothers and sisters. His father, Charles George Rex, an immigrant from England, was a carpenter who worked on some of Springfield's largest buildings. Ill health struck early in the younger Charles' life when at the age of three he came down with polio which left him paralyzed from the waist down and partially paralyzed in his right hand, thereby virtually confining him to a wheel chair for most of his life, although for a time he was able to use heavy braces and crutches. The polio had also caused severe scoliosis of his spine with the result that he was often in great pain.

In spite of these handicaps, it became obvious in childhood that Rex was gifted with extraordinary intelligence and musical ability. Due to the complete lack of educational facilities for the handicapped in his area, his early schooling and musical studies were virtually self-taught. Nonetheless, he was an avid reader from an early age and started writing poetry in his teenage years. He managed to learn piano and violin and acquired a remarkable amount of proficiency on these instruments in spite of the partial paralysis of his right hand, enough so that he played violin as a member of a local orchestra.

It was in his vocal abilities that Rex first achieved success. With the financial backing of a patron of the arts who recognized his talent, starting at the age of eighteen, he studied voice in Springfield for five years with RCA

Victor recording artist Royal Dadmun. At this time, Rex started writing poetry, a handwritten note on a penciled manuscript revealing that his first poem was "The Thrush's Song," written in 1928. He later started giving solo vocal recitals as a baritone, earning praise from newspaper critics for his "volume and unusual beauty of tone." Dadmun himself wrote to him, "I count on you as an exponent of whatever value my ideas may have." Rex was also a vocal soloist for the Travelers Insurance Symphony Orchestra under conductor Moshe Paranov, co-founder and dean of the Hartt School of Music, on WTIC AM radio out of Hartford, Connecticut, for the NBC Red Radio Network.

In 1935, Rex married his first wife, Miriam, and moved to New York City where he studied voice with well-known vocal instructor, Alfredo Martino, who later made him his first assistant. Eventually, he had his own studio and an assistant teacher through Martino's helpfulness and also collaborated on a book with Martino entitled "Today's Singing." According to personal notes, Rex also often went through periods where he would write a poem a day, a favorite form being the sonnet.

His ultimate ambition being music composition, however, he came to the conclusion that he needed a formal education, and so, with no previous academic schooling, he finished high school in nine months and entered Amherst College, where he was a member of Theta Xi national social fraternity and Pi Kappa Lambda Honor Society. There he studied with American composer Ross Finney.

Rex later transferred to Rollins College in Winter Park, Florida, where after a little over three years he graduated in 1946 with both Bachelor of Music and Bachelor of Arts degrees while sustaining a 98% grade-point average as well as winning the college's highest award, the Algernon Sydney

Sullivan Award for outstanding achievement. After graduation, he became part of the music faculty of Rollins College for two years. During this time, he was also involved in a weekly radio program of dramatized plays for children for which he composed the music and acted.

After a divorce, Rex married his second wife, Betty, in 1948 with whom he had three children. In the early 1950s, he was director of bands and choruses for the Mt. Dora High School in Florida while continuing to compose music and poetry. Increasing ill-health during this time, however, started severely curtailing his musical activities with the result that after fulfilling some isolated commissions from the Florida Symphony and composing some short piano works, his musical life had to virtually cease, although he still continued to write poetry.

In 1964, Rex developed colon cancer that was cured by surgery. In 1966, the family broke up, and Rex moved to Tallahassee, Florida, to be near one of his sons who was attending Florida State University. Suffering from increasing depression, he barely survived a suicide attempt in August of 1970. After his recovery, he still continued to write poetry. He ultimately moved back to Springfield in 1972 and died of a stroke on April 23, 1973.

Charles Gordon Rex's children, Charles, Jr., Christopher, and Cathy, have carried on their father's musical tradition. Charles Rex (Jr.) became a concert violinist and was a first violinist in the Philadelphia Orchestra under Eugene Ormandy after graduating from Florida State University on a full scholarship. He was later the Associate Concertmaster of the New York Philharmonic under Zubin Mehta and Leonard Bernstein as well as serving as interim Concertmaster of the London Symphony Orchestra on a concert tour of England under Sir Colin Davis. Christopher Rex became a cellist and was also in the Philadelphia Orchestra after graduating from the Curtis

Conservatory. He later became the Principal Cellist of the Atlanta Symphony under Robert Shaw and Robert Spano, and also served as substitute Principal Cellist of the New York Philharmonic on a European concert tour by the NYP under Maestro Mehta. Cathy Rex was proficient on piano but decided not go into music professionally.

It is true that poet and composer Charles Gordon Rex's style of writing, finally being published in the 21st Century, is that of a bygone era, this being so because he was the product of the first half of the Twentieth Century with the bulk of his works being written in the 1930s and 1940s. His preferred form was the venerable sonnet. For other forms, a major influence was the poetry of A. E. Housman, many of whose poems Rex as a composer set to music. Thus it is unfortunate that during his own lifetime, he rarely bothered with the publication of either his poetry or his music, although a few of his poems did appear in such popular magazines of the time as *Good Housekeeping* and later in the intellectual journal, *First Things*. It is well known among musicians, however, that good music, no matter when it was written, will eventually find its place. As a pertinent example, Rex's "Song Cycle on A. E. Housman Poems" for soprano, string quartet, and piano, unheard since its premiere performance in 1946, was finally heard again over forty years later in 1987, and the reviewer for *The New York Times* called it "the most affective piece on the program." It is the hope of the editor that if there is value in the poetry of Charles Gordon Rex, it will find its place as well and that lovers of poetry will enjoy his work as represented in this volume.

The Poems

LISTEN TO MY SONG

Listen to my song, gaze not upon me.
My spirit long has broke these earthly chains.
My soul has found at last a greener valley
And fetters not itself with human gains.

My body, broken, would have tried to bind me
Had not my mind reached out to nobler things.
Now I am conscious of nought else but beauty;
Forgetting self, it is my soul that sings.

THE LAST MAN

Restrained no more, the last rebelling man,
Alone as he had always wished to be,
Sole monarch of himself, with not a clan,
Nor tribe, nor state, nor nation left that he,
Protesting, must obey, has sat him down
Upon the last green acreage of sod
And woven of the pliant grass a crown
To show the rotted dead that he is God.

To show the dead his is the only face;
His thought the only consciousness; his eye
The only judge of substance or of space;
His skull the only congruence with sky.
And singing loud his praise he spends his breath,
Extinguishing the universe in death.

(Originally published in *First Things*)

THE PRODIGALS

I hope to kill the fatted calf somehow,
Before its youth is gone, and in its stead
There stands a lean and empty-uddered cow
From whom all festiveness has fled;
Before its innocence, naiveté,
Has, from neglect, been changed to dull, morose,
Unfeeling gloom that holds all joy at bay,
And with its bones it pierces skin drawn close.

I hope to pile the groaning board up high,
And importune the prodigals to eat,
Ignore the Elder Brother standing by,
And give themselves completely to the meat.
But what if prodigals exist no more,
And all are Elder Brothers at the door?

(Originally published in *First Things*)

A CHILD OF SUMMER

I know what summer should be like to me,
A child of summer, born the day before.
There is a proper green for bush and tree,
And certain tints that flowers show; and, more
Than all, there is the smell of new-cut grass,
And sounds of insects, dull from too much sun;
The taste of sweat; the feel of winds that pass
Too slow through leaves to bend a single one.

And I try to tell you of my birth,
And what my native season should contain
Of sun upon a warm responsive earth,
Of sudden thunder and torrential rain.
Yet being told, what could you truly know
If you were born to honor sleet and snow?

ADVENTURE

The wind has bent the tussock grass,
And winnowed through the sand,
And flung it whispering on the pines
And in the shallow sea.

It's calm here, love; yet deep as deep
The sea that we seek now,
And we can't know how strong the wind
Until we slip the shore.

AMBITION

I want to build love note by note, --
A true, enduring chime;
Just as eternity was built, --
An aeon at a time.

AND THUS IT IS

I picked a rose;
With its fragrance I would linger.
Yet while I raised it to my lips,
It pricked my finger!

I saw the moon;
I raised my hand toward the sky.
And yet before I greeted her,
A cloud passed by!

And thus it is;
I do no know the reason why,
But should I think to sail a ship --
The wind would die!

AND WHEN I COME TO DIE

And when I come to die, if in solitude, let me not forget
How the wind blew free and clean across my life;
How the love of my friends came to me often in many ways.
Little memories I have now of their faces softened by time,
Always kindly now. A little lonely I am, a little sad.
If only when I am come to die it might not be in solitude!
For I am afraid. If only those that I love could come as I know
Them and stand by my side, smiling once more,
Then perhaps I would not weep.
It is a passing loneliness I know, for I have you
Whom I love more than the place that I am striving for
In the world, the things I am trying to do -- futile things.
The fire has burned low and I must sleep.
Tomorrow this sweet sadness will be gone
And I will have lost this tenderness.
The last ember has gone. The memories that have come to me
Tonight have gone.
Tomorrow will give me new joy and you whom I love.

ANNIVERSARY

    It is enough almost, that you and I
Have loved, and known the seasons of our years,
Have seen them all: the summer sun, the tears
    Of spring, the vague unrest of chilling sky,
    That half congealed in winter arches high
    At night about the rigid earth, or peers
At dawn through frosty, beetled brows, or nears
    The tops of trees at dusk as shadows die.

And we have known far more than poets sing
    Of tender looks and warm embraces, too;
    But still this fruit is not enough for such
    As we who seek a further blossoming.
Why should the past suffice for me and you
When all that can yet come is not too much?

ANOTHER

You could love me if you wanted;
You could love me, aye, you could.
If myself were but another,
You could love me, aye, you would.

You've another lad more handsome;
He it is your heart may fill.
Were I he, then all is other,
But I'm not nor never will.

Three do love, but two each other;
Two are happy, one alone.
In the sunlight, warm are the flowers;
In the shadow, chill is the stone.

ANOTHER SONG

My song you hear and then despair
To remember who was singing there;
But even as the echoes die,
Another song shall fill the air!

AS BEFORE

There's not a single thing to tell
Since grief passed by the door
And took the laughter all away
And left me as before.

The morning of it wore a smile,
Gave noon a cloudless air
That twilight found too burdensome
With stars too bright to bear.

Here now is dreadful midnight
With none around to say
What better sequence could have made
A finer yesterday.

AS ONE WHO WALKS

As one who walks along the yielding sand
And, fearful of the ocean, keeps a space
Between him and the tugging waves, his face
Turned straight ahead, ignoring their demand,
Nor swerves aside toward more substantial land
But firmly holds his course with steady pace,
Defies the sea, and deems it no disgrace
To run from what he does not understand,--

So parallel to you, a width between,
I share your walk, defiant of your love,
Preferring as I do the solid ground
And dangers that I know to those unseen.
Yet even so, in ways I know not of,
I may be seized, and drawn within, and drowned.

AUTUMN

The trees and sky play
Such sweet, elusive music today,
And lone am I
Under the singing sky;
None else heard
Save a bird
Who joyed to fling
Song-echoes on the wing.

The flaunted leaf
Means not grief
For dying things.
The brook sings,
Nor does it care
How crisp the air.

Lone am I
Under the singing sky.
None else heard,
Save a bird.
And I am glad,
For man is sad
At dying; not with me
Would he have heard brook and tree
And singing sky play
Sweet, elusive notes today.

THE AWAKENING

"It is not polite," I told him,
"To come noisily into my room
So early in the morning
And awaken me."

This morning he tiptoed in,
And with his lips close
To my ear whispered,
"Are you awake?"

There was a great shout of triumph
This afternoon as he raised a noble,
Lofty, slanty, rickety edifice --
Five feet toward the sky.

Tonight as I slept, his small hand
On my shoulder startled me awake.
In the half light, even as I spoke sharply to him,
I saw a deep concern:

Does he already know that someday
All his shouts, tears, and prayers
Will not get him a word
Of love or reproof?

After his hand has groped,
His eyes searched, his lips inquired --
Will he silently raise another edifice,
Symmetrical, this time to me?

AUTUMNAL EQUINOX

The long round lines of rain shine
The black streets and flick
The red leaves of the vine.

The wind tosses thin blue smoke
Over the wet roofs; and on the hill away
A fringe of maples that claw and choke
For breath the wind has sucked away.

Sidling, shoulder on the wind,
Grimacing at where he was before,
Clutching at a restless coat, a man
Gains shelter and grateful, slams the door.

BACHELORHOOD

What do I need -- that you, perhaps, may give --
More than the books I read, the food I eat,
The bed I lie on, or the hours I live
Beyond the reach of words? How incomplete
Is day and night for me with the gift
Of what I lack, and you alone possess,
Or say you do? And just how sure and swift
Would be the change from Now to Happiness?

To read a book was never meant for two,
Despite the seeming oneness of their thought;
And were sleep broken on a bed with you,
Then gone would be the very rest I sought.
Far better now your sweetness to deny
Then future angry word and sullen eye.

BENDING TREES

Whenever wind was bending trees at night
To break their backs and have them down to stay,
And branches rubbed the roof and leapt away
To carry with them boards that were not tight,
Then she would lie and whimper in her fright,
And pull the bed-clothes tighter in dismay
That she was all alone, with none to say,
"It's just the wind," and rise and strike a light.

Too often now the house was dark and still,
And he away as soon as chores were done;
Tonight the wind had pushed him down the hill,
And made him run who did not like to run.
He came and thought her fast asleep until
He sat upon the bed and saw the gun.

BLOW GENTLY

Blow gently, warm wind from the west,
Swing not too wild the songbirds' nest.
I've seen the care with which they build;
How every opening was filled,
How every straw and stick was laid.
Ah, with what love their home was made!

Then, blow you gently; someday will
Come newer voices, fresh and shrill
From fluffy things that writhe and squirm
And cease their crying for a worm
But only for an instant, then
Begin their hungry cry again.

And untired through summer days
The songbirds go their busy ways
And find no time to sit and sing,
Nor will they till the coming spring.
And then, O warm wind from the west,
They shall build another nest.

BOOKS

The clock strikes too oft for my content,
And fear comes in persistent here
Where never it was meant.

I shall not sleep tonight. Time goes on.
For me, there is much to see
From now till after dawn.

And even in day devoid of dark
I peer, nor even pause to hear,
However sweet, the lark.

I must turn endless pages of thought
Again to speak with vanished men,
And seek what they have sought.

I must know and feel and strive to know.
No bend is in my road, no end;
Nor is there where I go.

I grieve with those who went before
What time, as fleeting as a rhyme
Sounds sweetly, then no more.

O gorge on all that feeds my mind,
Delight my hunger day and night,
Nor leave a crumb behind.

What then shall be for me at last?
A kiss is what you mean I miss?
Does that comprise my fast?

What other fast then may I know?
For clear it is that love is here
More deep than I could show.

Then song of bird? Linnet? Lark?
They sing more clear on phantom wing
Awakened in the dark.

The dream or real for me is blent
To one, the same in shade or sun;
I read and am content.

THE BOWERY

The years had added the furrows' creases
Like the lines of a fork drawn through buttery grass.
His crooked fingers hackled his beard,
And the wanton wind at his anguish jeered.
Give it no thought then,
Let it alone;
Yours is the warm flesh,
His is the bone.
His trousers stood there with bended knee,
And the legs were ampleness, roomy and free.
His coat in back could never be straight
For his spine had bowed like an arched gate.
Arc in your walking,
Give him no heed;
Pitying, talking
Isn't the deed.
He drops his string in the frosty grate
And he sniffs as he hauls in his prize -- or fate.
He sells his booty for fifty cents
And he's off to procure his peculiar defense.
Write to the mayor
When you are free.
Do it for conscience.
Do it for me.

THE BOY THAT HE WAS

The boy that he was has gone away,
A trace hardly left in the man of today.
The boy that he was had laughing eyes
And a ringing shout, a happy surprise
For the smallest thing that brought him joy.
Oh, is he gone, that carefree boy?
Though his eyes have grown hard with a worldly chill,
Is he not that same boy still?

CATHY SUE

Two hands,
Dimpled and small,
Reach up to find my nose,
Move it softly, and thereby touch
My heart.

Two eyes,
Steady and blue,
Look at me and question
About life, but, instead, teach me
Of love.

"This is,"
I tell her, "All
I know of life: Create
In storms and calms, for then it is
You live!"

If she,
As she is now,
Could know what I have said,
She would understand; but later--
Who knows?

For fear
Might someday come,
And her steps, unsteady,--
But not because walking is new,--
Might falter.

But if
I, myself, am
Brave, then shall she also,
And free to choose. Thus I must teach
Myself.

CHANGE

I could give you cool treatment for the sting of it;
I could turn quickly from you and walk to the nearest exit.
I could, I say--
If you were not you, and this were yesterday.

CHANT FOR SPRING

Come....
Come feel Spring with me;
The kind warm air, and see
Bright flowers and new-dressed trees,
And more than these.

Rise....
Come rise and joy with me
In earth and sky, and see
Life waking in the bladed sod,
And more than that,--know God!

CHRISTMAS

How bright the house was when at Christmas time
They trimmed the tree, the largest one in town,
And stacked the children's gifts beneath the boughs
That bent almost with countless ornaments
Of red and blue, with lighted angels robed
In porcelain and haloed with gold wire –
God's helpers flanked by Santa's gnomes – all these
Climbed upward through the countless colored bulbs
That finally diminished at the top
To just one upright, aromatic branch.
A neighbor always placed the tinseled star,
For neither he nor she could reach that far.

CINQUAINS

Rain is
Upon water
Like small, silver hammers
That play sweet, fairy music on
Wavelets.

The moon
Is a lovely
Lady, whose train of clouds
Is held from the dust of earth by
A star.

Seagulls,
Flying in the
Sunlight, are foam-flecks spewed
From the lips of waves, maddened by
The wind.

Beneath
The pale-green sea
Are mermaids, pink coral,
And dreamless men with seaweed in
Their hair.

CLOUDS AT SUNSET

How peacefully move
The softly floating clouds,
Turned crimson and gold by the sun
Which, even as a leaf in autumn,
Turns to colors in its dying.

CONTENTMENT

Ah! Never will I be content
Till all my worldly goods are spent.
Then will I love both friend and foe,
Not reason why they came or went.

A CONVERSATION IN THE RAIN

Lonely, drenched tree,
What do you know of wonders,
Of God and rains and thunders?
You bow your head to ev'ry breeze
And stand aloof from other trees;
Your branches tremble at the blow
Of ev'ry drop of rain or snow.

Then said the tree:
"I've stood here for an hundred years
And held the birds and known their fears;
I've lived when others passed away.
I've seen the world in bright array
Change to cold and sparkling white
And heard the wind that howls at night.

"I've felt these things time and again
And I have found that God IS rain,
For rain refreshes thirsting flowers.
An act of love is drenching showers;
An act of love, an act of God
Are both the same to we of the sod.

"I tremble, not because I'm weak;
I bow my head for I am meek,
Accepting all that comes my way
And shelt'ring those who know dismay.
I feel His power in every leaf
And so for me there is no grief.

"Stupid, drenched man,
What do you know of wonders,
Of God and rains and thunders?
You don't know much at all, I'd say --
You've stood here in the rain all day!"

COUPLETS - A FEW READINGS

(After all, what can you lose?)

When I count up the things I've lost,
The benefits out-weigh the cost.

****

The man that I once thought to be
Would not have been a bit like me.

****

Dreaming Youth! How vain its boasts!
For deeds to come, there are no toasts!

****

Philosophy, of charming word,
Is sometimes tried – more often heard.

****

A brilliant speaker may just be
A man who thinks the same as we.

****

I'd like to think all men were good:
If I were, too, why – then I would!

****

Security will dull the wit;
A little danger sharpens it!

****

No man has gone to the poorhouse yet
For having something that was hard to get.

****

The wrinkle of Trouble with which we cope
Can be pressed out with the iron of Hope!

****

Inspiration comes from one
Who praises work when it is done.

****

It's often well that we don't make
The roads that we decide to take.

****

If I relived my life, why, then –
I'd do the same fool things again!

****

The pride of achievement and of wealth
Cannot compare with the joy of health.

****

This world would not be such a mess
If man would know things – not just guess!

****

From wishes that I didn't get
I've learned that I don't need them yet!

COURAGE

When it is morning
And courage is yours,
Wait not for the warning
Cry of fear.

Heed only the triumphant light,
Not cringing shadows.
And dim not your sight
With a tear.

THE CRICKET

The mournful cricket's chirping
His faint, persistent song.
He sings the while, usurping
The vestments of the strong;

For, though he would be scornful,
His play, he knows, is through.
I say that he is mournful –
I know, for I am, too.

His fear-filled soul is quaking,
Too soon the snow will come;
His notes are weak and shaking,
Too soon he's stricken dumb.

The drowsy night is fleeting;
It will not last for long,
So I will keep repeating
With him his ancient song.

I loathe the coming coldness,
I love the warmth of spring;
O let us in all boldness
Forget our grief and sing!

THE DAWN

I've watched the dawn so many times
Devouring the sky,
That resurrection seems a hurt
That makes me fear to die.

THE DEAD

The dead exist in memories;
Their world in him who cares;
In him who, when he joins them,
Destroys his realm and theirs.

DEPARTURE

You have shared all my joys
And lightened the sorrows
I've known in time past.
If there are no tomorrows
With you, there's no joy,
And other sorrows I'll know
Will never compare
To the one when you go.

DESTINY

Today I live and know the will
Of destiny; and cannot fill
My life with what tomorrow brings;
Tomorrow is tomorrow still.

THE DINNER PARTY

I'll give a dinner party
Soon after I am dead,
And not a relative will come
Nor any friends. Instead
The guests, all uninvited,
Will worm their way inside,
And they'll be quite attached to me,
Soon after I have died.
And I'll be known for miles around
For generosity
As, silently, I tell my guests,
"The food is all on me!"

DISCONSOLATE

Oh, I would like to find a girl who sings;
A girl who thinks not of material things,
A girl who bathes in calm, ethereal springs.

I would have her kind and minus frown,
With golden hair and eyes of limpid brown,
With lovely form and hands as soft as down.

Oh, I will know her, strange though it may seem;
A girl like this I saw once in a dream,
And then she faded, leaving but hope's gleam.

Perhaps I'll find her near the rolling sea,
Or on the land beneath a shady tree:
But if I did, she wouldn't care for me!

THE DOOR

The door is there,--
What lies beyond?

Man may only knock
And hurry back,
Or else remain
Until the door
Is opened wide,
And going through
Know the answer --
And keep forever still.

DREAMERS

How clever must one be to tell
The toll that May with all its blossoms takes
Of hearts too young to recognize
The phantasies one lilac cluster makes?

As clever as a man must be
Who would with words the poppy dreamer wake
From worlds too wonderful to show
On canvas, or in ways the poets take.

For of the hearts thus held in thrall,
Not one but may be judged as lost to such
Firm stuff the learned say is real;
But in their state, it does not matter much.

DREAMS OF YOUTH

Strong, young and pure you are as summer dawn
That rises from the deepness of the sea
And strews its tender colors out upon
Cool waves grown wiser in eternity.

Dreams of golden days are rising with you;
But you can't really know that colors fade,
Nor understand that suns rise in the blue
And must thenceforth reflect in dawns new-made.

Hold fast your dreams, and let them ever shine
From out your eager haunting eyes like stars;
Drain them of all joy -- I did not mine --
For plucked too soon from out the heart leaves scars.

Fling back your head and know the morning truth;
Stretch out young arms and greet the ancient sea;
Throw wide the portals of fair lovely youth,
But hold the dreams of youth eternally!

E FINITO

I watch you go,
Find no tears
In parting, know
Little of a meeting
On some far day.

Yet if you tried to point
Your goal, or could,
I doubt if I could find you,
Or would.

FAREWELL TO UNBORN FAME

If someone should tell the world
To look here,
I'm sure it would shine me up and put me
Where I'd show.

I would sit tailor fashion
Upon the sideboard
And smile in my silveriness as if
I were proud.

And hard-faced cold people
Would come by,
Still with their coat and hats on,
Some with galoshes.

They'd see my smile which would try to say,
"Let's be friendly."
Some of them would pick me up, turn me over and over
And say, "Humph!"

I'd be scared, I know,
And shed tears
Most of the time if someone told the world
To look here.

So I won't say anything,
But better still,
I'll put on coat, hat, and galoshes and walk by
With the others.

THE FAINT HEART

She goes dancingly,
Tripping entrancingly
Down the road to the tree by the mill.
I go blund'ringly,
Often quite thund'ringly,
Longing to speak, yet with her strangely still.

I wish that I did not feel clumsy with her,
My love with the small, fairy feet;
I cannot be stalwart and handsome, I know,
But I'd like to feel graceful and neat.

With men I am eloquent, poised and commanding,
But she has a glance that seems reprimanding;
Perhaps it will not be so when I confess
My love for the Fairest and she answers, "Yes!"

I can hardly wait!
I hear the garden gate
Swing on its hinges with protesting squeak!
Soon she will come to me.
What will her answer be? --
Oh, I shall not have the courage to speak!

FIRST BORN

This is my son and hers who bore the weight
Of him through tedious, heavy hours until
With sweat and pain was opened up the gate
And he thrust out into the first faint chill
Of dawn and his first consciousness; my son
And hers, and yet not ours to own, to clutch
As drowning men at straws; or shield as one
Afraid that life will always prove too much.

He is himself, unique, belonging to
Himself and that great force that gave him birth,
And answerable only to the true
Existences of heaven and of earth.
This is our son to have for such a length
Of time as will suffice to give him strength.

(Printed courtesy of Hearst Magazine Media, Inc.)

FIRST LOVE

I remember an autumn.
Red oak leaves
Crackling on the ground;
A few acorns,
Dry -- hollow;
A warm sun,
Red behind pine trees.
Yet cold was the stone bench upon which we sat,
Cold as the graves
Set in disorderly array about us.
But warm were the lips of my first love
Whom I kissed
One Sunday in autumn long ago.

FOR CERTAIN TALK

For certain talk, the only time is night
When sleep is near enough to make a dream
Not very different from real, or seem
The same if there is none, or little light
To jar the eye and startle late fright
The friendly brain; friendly in its esteem
For self, and any others it may deem
As not a friend -- when handicapped by sight.

Night is a dark and wooly blanket shared;
A curtain drawn against who might come in
If it were day; a room where what is cared
About the most is kept; a sable skin
For warmth and drowsiness; it is the bared
Untutored soul in point of pious sin.

FOUR BOOKS

There are four books
On my shelf.
Taken together, they are
Myself.

The first is what
I know:
Things I am sure are, or are not,
So.

What I think
Is in the second one:
All that I have, or have not,
Done.

The third is what
I feel:
Love that is, or is not,
Real.

The fourth -- how I
Behave:
What regularly I do, or do not,
Crave.

Here they are
And read them slow:
Then what I am you may, or may not,
Know.

FRAGRANCE

I bring you a rose, my darling.
The tender lips of the morning
Have passed, and left their sweetness
Upon its sleeping petals.

So may they sleep, my darling,
Until the touch of your hands
Shall wake them and their lovely fragrance
Enter my heart.

FRIENDS

If love I give to my friends,
I keep them – new and old.
But friends no more are they
If I give gold!

FROM HERE TO THERE

From here to there is measured by a span
Of time, or breath, or call it what you will;
It is the distance known by any man,
Who conscious of the now, but moving, still
Is cognizant of what may come, and goes
With slower tread, or wasteful of his stride,
As need may hasten or defer repose,
Like for a willing, or unwilling, bride.

And though defined, how can the judging eye
Reflect with any hope of certainty
The length of what may well be truth or lie,
Since here and there is vague proximity?
Far, far ahead we hope may be the mark,
And yet, another step, and all is dark!

FROM MY NEW HOUSE

From my new house I've wondered
How looked the town,
White house, grey house, brown,
When from my window down
I looked this summer long.
Thick hedge, foliage of tree
Lent intriguing mystery
To all I could not see.
Now this obliging clime
Reveals the town to me,
But frugally,
And one leaf at a time.

FULFILLMENT

The tiny bloom
Faced the hot sky.
Parched, dry,
It watched one cloud
Swell to shroud
The sun and spread its wrack.

The rain came earthward
And broke the blossom's back.

THE GAMBLER

Tomorrow, Love, I've sworn
That when I rise,
I'll know the passion
Slumb'ring in your eyes.

If this be right,
Then God will let me wake;
You see, My Love,
The chances that I take?

GEMINI

"There were two of me, you know;
It was not I whom she let go."

"Strange, indeed, she never knew
The one that you insist was you."

GIFTS

A song, O bird, from you to me,
And a breath of salt from the shining sea;
A scent of pine from a pungent tree
And my love returning.

These are the gifts that I will share
With my love: a place in the open air,
A moon that glides up a star-hung stair,
And a campfire burning.

Great are the gifts that have come to me;
The flash of a wing from a swaying tree,
The shatter of silver from a breaking sea
On golden sand.

And I will share them all with one
Who thrills at earth and sky and sun;
I'll drop them all, withholding none
Into her hand.

A GREATER FEAR

A greater fear than that of death
Is life, that quickener of breath,
Against whose fires we scorch our hands,
Encircle freedom with its bands
Of duty, let its surge deride
Our honor, hopes, and even pride;
Cold pride which spells the soul's decay
And proves our very essence clay.

We fear the night, to enter sleep,
To slack the constant vigil. Keep
Our fingers on its pulse to know
Always that the conscious glow
Still shines with that ephemeral tint
Which flows about us like the glint
Of sun and summer, bird and stream,
That we may dream our silver dream;

And dreaming live and living dream,
Hands clammy; from the darker beam
　　We fear delay, yet if it came
　　Nearer, then with fiercer flame
　　Would our very blood run hot;
　　We call it forth and want it not:
Complcte the garment stitch by stitch,
　　But ravel it or wear it -- which?

THE GUEST

November washed the world this morn
And hung it out to dry,
Brushed the cobwebs from the thorn
And tidied up the sky.

Upon the woodland hearth she laid
A sumac flame to burn,
And for the mantel hills, she made
A centerpiece of fern.

Then on her charming bosom hung
A chain of water falls;
And thus, with mist about her flung,
Walked down the Autumn halls.

She had, indeed, a guest to meet,
Austere, in crackling white;
Whose frowns were fierce and smiles were fleet,
Who's come in dark of night.

And he would beg her to condone
　　His forwardness. And might
He have her domain for his own,
　　And could he stay the night?

But, ah, he had a fickle tread
　　That led him oft to stray,
So she would blush an oak-leaf red
　　And go her Autumn way.

And she was right -- I after heard
　　Two lured him forth, this king:
The one a siren warbling bird,
　　The other – Mistress Spring!

HALF A JOURNEY

I made but half a journey,
And much against my will;
The way was up a tortured path
Ingrained against a hill.

The summit proved itself too far,
The road too sharp with stones;
Enough my flesh, no reason for
A sacrifice of bones.

I now seek small endeavors
For sensitivity:
The changing of the seasons
Is hurt enough for me.

HALF A LOAF

What strangers say in friendly pleasantry
    Would be for lovers incongruity:
      With lovers it is famine or feast,
    A silent most or else a wordy least.

HAPPY TO HIS ARMS

Her eyes were bright, yes, that she knew,
Her figure lovely, slim;
Her hair was dark and waved just right,
For she was meeting HIM!

And though she really wasn't scared,
Her heart was acting queer,
For he was handsome, fair and tall,
And looked a perfect dear.

She hadn't really wanted to
Meet him till today;
They'd seen each other once or twice
But in a casual way.

Besides, if people really knew,
They might not let her go,
And he was so insistent that
She mustn't now say "no."

A final glance into the glass
Assured her of her charms,
Then silently she left the house, --
Went happy to his arms.

******

And that's the way she'd tell it, too,
If given but the chance;
I'm sure that is the way she died,
For Grandma loved romance...

HAPPINESS

Happiness, how vainly sought
By those who think it something to receive.
Happiness, it is the thought
That will a fellow mortal's pain relieve.
Happiness is wingéd shoes
With which the feet of him who loves are shod;
Happiness comes of itself
To every soul that strives to walk with God!

HISTORY

The people of another day
Move silently within my head
In stiffly starched and doleful dress
When History is read.

They always speak in learned words,
A manner different from mine.
I cannot quite believe they lived,
Those phantoms of a phantom line.

But story people breathe and laugh,
Are warm and very like me;
They never say things wise and sage,
Or -- so alive -- I do not see.

A page of some far future book
One picture may contain of me;
Thus note -- I live and foolish am,
All you who read that History!

HUMAN NATURE

Human Nature --
So are called
All the weaknesses of men.
If they're noble,
If they're fine,
'Tis not Human Nature then.

But I like to
Think of it
As a little of the two;
Human Nature
to be false,
Human Nature to be true

A HYMN OF PRAISE

I know there is no power great as He
Who paints the colors of the changing sea;
Who tears the veils from those whose clouded sight
Wear the somber vestments of the night.
There is no power great as He who made
The daisy foam upon a sea of jade;
Who smilingly set mountains in the sun
Where reflects the light of day begun.

Oh, great is He who made immortal Life.
Who builded souls within the womb of strife;
Who first conceived the thought of making Man;
The Being that defeats dark Lethe's plan.
I drink my fill from out Life's flowing bowl
And loud the praises of His might extol!

I CAN SEE THE SKY

From my porch and from my doorway
I can see the sky;
Blue it is till some cloud galleon
Sails sedately by.

Sometimes my patch of azure bright
Is cloven by the robin's flight.
Then at night, my bit of blue
Changes to a different hue;
Velvet soft, with diamonds set
Gleaming from a heart of jet.

With such beauty overhead,
I need not look at living dead
That pass below me in the street
With chalk-white face and leaden feet,
Though they need beauty just as I
Need my bit of sapphire sky.

From my porch and from my doorway
I can see the sky;
Blue it is, and I must keep it
Or, though living, die.

I DIED A YEAR AGO TODAY

I died a year ago today,
Yet I am breathing still;
It would have been the darker way
Could I have worked my will.

But there were those who had the whim
That I continue thus;
Still nothing in the interim
Has made it worth the fuss.

(This poem was written in 1971, approximately one year after the author's unsuccessful suicide attempt.)

I WILL ASK ONLY THAT

"Let me touch your hand; I will ask only that."
"Here is my hand; do you not feel its warmth?"
"Let me lay my lips upon the softness of yours;
I will ask only that."
"Here are my lips; do you not feel their moist
quivering?"
"And your eyes -- let me read their sweet secret;
I will ask only that."
"My eyes are brimming with what has long overflowed
my heart."
"Alas! You have given all; now I cannot ask
for more!"

I WOULD NOT TARRY MORE

And so I thought I would not tarry more
And on vain pursuits firmly closed the door.
But sailing then, someone there was who said,
"The wind is fair; why gaze you back to shore?"

IF I COULD KNOW

If I could know for just a brief time the full beauty of your
eyes; for just the merest space feel the warmth of their
loveliness shining upon me; take to myself for one moment
the humid glow of life deep within them -- what would transpire
in the smoldering fires that still burn under the grey ashes
of my life?

Might it not be that a sudden burst of emotion would rush into
a flame of fire, bright and fierce?

Or would such warmth as they provoked lull me, and let me sink
deep into a dream of summer languor where colors and sounds
create a pleasure almost too great to bear?

O my Beautiful One, whether there shall come fire or a quiet
dreaming, let me have my fill of the dark, endless wonders
which are your eyes.

IF ONLY

If only you had not been
So hauntingly beautiful,
Like pale mist, tinted;
Light faint music, singing.

If only you had not been
So tenderly kind,
Like soft hands, clinging;
Like cool water on parched lips.

Perhaps then, my beloved,
I could have lived as men do
Who have not seen mirages
That shimmer and lure and vanish;

Who have not seen sunlight on wavelets
Or the flight of the eagle who returns,
As now do I, to bare, brown earth
And arid wastes.

I would have liked to stay, my darling,
But better to have flown.
I would have liked to live, my darling,
But better to have known!

IF YOU SPEAK

If you speak, ever so silently,
I will hear;
If you weep, ever so softly,
One crystal tear,
I will know.
If you laugh, ever so lightly,
It will go
A bright arrow, ever so swiftly,
As from a bow;
Straight will it fly.
If I am laid, ever so deeply,
Under the sky,
The flowers will sway, ever so gracefully
At your sigh;
The trees shall be stirred.
And if you pray, ever so little,
Just one word,
Then will I hear, ever so gently,
What He heard often before.
And I will come, ever so quietly,
Across the floor
Of years, and ever so patiently
Wait for the door
To open.

IMAGERY

Sometimes I'm large,
Bigger than all:
Tree, garden, garden wall --
Mountain even.

Today I loosed the bonds
Of Imagery,
And, being free,
My mind soared very high,

But I don't mind.
I've always wanted to
Reach the blue,
Yet stand on earth.

Here now am I,
Looking down,
At my feet earth, brown,
On my head -- the sky!

IMMORTALITY

A tiny thing is all it takes
To tell us of the world:
Just give a bean away to earth
And get a bean unfurled.

And quite as simple is the tale
Of immortality:
One flower dies, another lives,
Connected by the bee.

If this be comfort, I am glad
It mitigates the dread;
But for myself, I shall admit
That when I'm dead. I'm dead.

IMPLACABLE

I'd wanted oft to talk with him;
Now know how it would be
To try make pliable with words
A block of masonry.

IN SEARCH OF TRUTH

I must not doubt
The future,
Nor think about
The past;
Nor cast
Away the prophesying
Of my friends.
Dying
Will not make amends
If I fail;
A ship does not sail
If it unloads
But half its cargo;
A spark explodes
Gunpowder
If it is good.

I must lift the hood
Of despair,
And dare
To ride
The rising tide
Of faithlessness
To the goal and desire
I set for myself,
And find the blue fire
Of truth
That, for Age and Youth,
Burns along the way
Of today.

IMPRISONMENT

Imprisonment requires no walls.
Far sterner than stone
Are streets traversed to monotony.

Fingers pressing hard on strings
Demand similar sounds
Combining into static symphonies
That one day close the ears entire to sound.

Days are rigid bars
Following each on each
To paucity and dearths;
A phalanx of stagnant years.

Sounds – identical – non-vibrant –
Weld into solid silence – endless.
Non da capo al fine.

INCOGNITO

I've seen satyrs,
Who at other times
Play the double flute,
Working in boiler factories;

And dryads,
Who know how to weave
And sway soft bodies,
Riveting steel plates;

And fawns,
Who sometimes sleep drunkenly
In sylvan glades,
Send out tools from the stockroom.

Yes, I've stumbled
On the most unexpected people!

JESUS OF NAZARETH

Jesus came
To Pilate's court
In seeming shame.

With silent strength
He answered not
Till at length

Him they hung
On a cross,
Him they stung

With scornful words.
And then two thieves,
Like mournful birds,

They hanged beside
Him who came
To reside

In the flesh,
That he might
Tear the mesh

That did bind
And ensnare
Mortal mind.

Jesus came
To reveal
One great name.

And for this
Death and blame
Were his rewards

Here on earth;
But in the place
To which he rose

In his re-birth,
He shall be
Infinity,
Power and Peace.

LAUGHTER

The man who has learned to laugh with the gods,
Even though at himself,
Has become one of them.

THE LAST BLOOM
A Sonnet Cycle

I

Sometimes when winter snow was piled waist high
And evergreens tossed handfuls to a wind
That flung them violently toward the sky
And dropped them with a hiss when they had thinned
To powder, and still others flecked with ice
Were dashed to bits against the window pane
Until it seemed that glass would not suffice
To keep out both the wind and frozen rain,

She straightened up a moment lost in snow
To rest her back and let the shovel down
That filled was half her weight, before the slow
And stubborn path would start again toward town.
She wondered then at all that she went through
To do the things her husband could not do.

II

She stamped her boots and left them at the door,
And stood a moment, waiting, half afraid
To meet the warmth that always hugged the floor,
And always cramped her toes when she had laid
Her socks aside, and always crushed her hands
With air so thick that underneath the fold
Of knitted cap and crease of scarf were bands
Of sweat although she shivered from the cold.

And yet the house was warm because of her,
For she it was who carried every bit
Of coal or stick of wood, and logs that were
Too heavy to be carried she would split.
She turned the knob and slowly went inside
To find the fire she feared had long since died.

III

Queer how at times she felt life passed her by,
That she, asleep and dreaming, missed the show,
And loneliness would often make her cry
As, when a child, she heard the raucous slow
Calliope retreat to distant tents
That housed the wonders of the world inside,
The wonders that but symbolized expense
To those in whom adventuring had died.

Back there were reasons; here she thought of none.
For all she asked was given as the ring
And lamp once gave to him who ordered done
The deeds that brought him wealth and made him king.
But getting what she asked was not the same
As getting what she wished but did not name.

IV

Once, at the end of winter, when the spring
Was turning snow to dirty mounds of gray,
And flooding meadows, bare of pasturing,
And country roads were beds of yellow clay,
She left the house in sullen rage and went
Without a turn to right or left straight through
The tussock grass that, brown and dead, was bent
By months of snow, toward where the distant blue

Of hazy hills was not too far to yield
To willful feet, nor yet so far they could
Recede beyond the farthest wood or field
As studded peaks and higher mountains would.
She reached their sides on which the highway wound
But hitched for home -- the longest way around.

V

He was not well the day that she ran off
And left him all alone until at dawn
She tiptoed in and listened to him cough
Before she shook the grate from which had gone
The slightest trace of either warmth or flame
That meant so much to him who had a dread
Of cold so great that when the winter came
He only left the fire to go to bed.

She felt no pity for him as she tore
The latest issue of a magazine
That lay a crumpled wad upon the floor
In strips to start the fire; the littered scene
But served to make her anger t'ward him rise
That what she read should make him criticize.

VI

When finally the doctor let him sit
Beside the window in an easy chair,
The grass was green and mating birds could flit
Once more in privacy through trees that, bare
In winter, simply meant a place to perch
And rest between the dusk and frozen dawn,
But in the spring -- a chamber and a church
Where songs and bird devotionals went on.

She sat nearby, her arm upon the sill,
And smoothed her dress, and then began to tell
The things the neighbors did when he was ill,
And how they worked so hard to keep her well.
She talked of household chores for half a day
Then brought him all the bills there were to pay.

VII

The smile he wore was with her through the night,
A disembodied grin that, Cheshire-wise,
Stayed on long after he was lost to sight
Who stamped it on the retina of eyes
Long unaccustomed now to seeing smiles
Of any kind upon a face grown stern,
A face that seemed impossible for wiles
To soften, or for bitter words to burn

To angry red, or joy to animate,
Or happiness to hide the lines of care
Etched deep; if not impossible, too late
For her who did not know why they were there.
She hated him not even knowing why;
Yet even so, she feared that he might die.

VIII

Then she recalled when what he took for love
 Was in his eyes and pounded in his breast,
  How he had sought relief and felt above
   The guardians of morals and their test
    For chastity; their jealously and crass
     Denial of a higher law that weaves
No binding, snaring webs in new spring grass,
 Nor banishes the mating birds like thieves.

And she could see again the shattered look
 That made him set his face and veil his eyes
When she, unmoved and passionless, forsook
 The cruel pretense that lures and then denies.
  She had insisted that if they were wed --
But when they were, she never shared his bed.

IX

Long, long ago, it seemed to her, the moon
    Was shining just as it was now, but such
Things as it then looked on were gone too soon
    For her to feel that they had mattered much;
    Yet somewhere buried deep in what she was
        Existed faintly what she tried to be,
        Existed as a sunken cargo does
When they have died who sent the ship to sea.

She drew the shade to hold the darkness in
    From where the moon imperiled it outside,
And saw once more her husband's vacant grin,
An absent smile from which all love had died.
    She strove to shut the image out, to keep
    Her eyes closed tightly 'til she fell asleep.

X

So slowly had the silence come, that now
Sometimes the days would pass with just a word
Or two exchanged; the kind that would allow
The one to nod their head if they had heard,
Or make no answer if they disagreed.
And often he was silent when he chose
To let the other's presence fill no need
For company, or else he yawned and rose

The moment that the other spoke and went
Upstairs and softly closed the door that led
Into his room, and stood a moment, bent
As though he strove to hear what had been said.
And each would wonder how they stood the strain
Of silence as the other probed their brain.

XI

He sat across the table with his book,
    Oblivious of her and of the food
He ate, nor did he lift his eyes and look
    Directly at her; nor did she intrude
    Upon the walled-in city of his mind
    That had no gates for her or anyone,
She thought, at least no gates that she could find
Or thoughts of trying made her want to run.

    She rose abruptly, took her plate away,
    And slid it clattering along the sink
    As though the noise itself sufficed to say
    The things her anger often made her think.
Her tear, she thought, might force him to look up.
He moved but once -- to push aside his cup.

XII

The grass was cool and damp beneath her feet
As barefoot in the dark she crossed the lawn
And sat upon the splintered, rustic seat
That faced the window where he sat till dawn
And wrote the things he used to read to her
When she could still pretend to understand
And cared enough to say how fine they were,
How well he read, and gently touched his hand.

She still was watching when his light went out
Near dawn, and not a breath of air had stirred
All night until it seemed the heat was wrapped
Around her, -- her who always said whatever word
She knew would keep him distant and enraged
And keep her passion secret, unassuaged.

XIII

She did not go to bed, but got her shoes
And walked across the field where meadow grass
Stood motionless until, when she would choose
To step, it bent itself to let her pass,
Then sprang erect again to brush her knees,
Pull at her skirt, and stand up tall once more,
Unmoving as the distant line of trees
Which marked the hill that she had climbed before

When anger drove as now her passion did
To seek relief in distance or to spurn
Her body's needs, ignoring ones she hid.
Unmindful, she would soon or late return,
Yet why she ran or why these things were so
She could not guess, nor did she want to know.

XIV

The house was dark and lifeless as the air
Itself when she came back to him; and yet
Not back to him exactly, but to where
The world would be unchanged, and every threat
Of day that only hours ago seemed all
That she could bear would not be near as hard
As anything she knew. The stubborn wall
Was down, and she more vanquished than men are

Who sell their countries' secrets for a song
And fear the law, or fear themselves the most
For having done what they were much too strong
To do, or so they thought. And now a ghost
Is there, a skeleton to hide, a stain
To scrub, and hands that will be washed in vain.

XV

She found but little comfort in her bed.
It was not cool nor white enough to soothe
Her restless limbs, and often she was led
To rise and fluff the pillow and to smooth
Unwrinkled sheets, to pull and tug and bind
Them taut around the mattress and to lie
More troubled than ill, unable now to find
Relief in sleep and too afraid to cry.

She lived again her watching in the night,
Her walking through the clinging grass and hay
Toward hills that, wanton in the growing light,
Flung shadows like flat garments turning gray;
And trees were much too high for her to tell
As she looked up if one or two leaves fell.

XVI

When she awoke, she lay a space or two
And watched a spider spin a silver fringe
Across the window screen to where askew
The shutter hung upon a broken hinge.
She suddenly remembered how the paint
Had blistered on the house, and here and there
Was peeling off 'til at a distance faint
As far-off rain, the wood showed. Trees were bare,

And when she raised herself, she saw the lawn,
Unkempt and straggly like a mad man's hair,
And noted in the disappearing dawn
The last bloom in her flower bed had gone,
Suppressed by overbearing weeds grown thick.
Then she recalled, and all at once was sick.

LIBERATION

I have sung so long in bondage
That a little freedom may paint
New dream colors which will be
As ephemeral and inconsistent as sunlight
Shining on the wings of a dragonfly.

I have flown in freedom a little way.
Yet even now my heart longs for the temple
Wherein I may seclude myself and release
My thoughts in true liberty.

LAST DAY OF JUNE

I came to realize today
That June had gone her lovely way,
And I, not knowing,
Had missed the emerald of her hills,
The meadows that she sweetly fills
With flowers, blowing.

Not before has it been so,
That she should come and blush and go
And I not see.
Ever have I danced ahead
To paths where she her way would tread
And come to me.

I'd go with her to ocean sands
And catch her scarf of colored bands
The breeze had blown.
And now it came to me today
That she had gone her lovely way
And I'd not known.

But I will sing a song to her
With note of pine and breath of fir,
A joyous tune.
Someday she will return to me
With golden sands and bluer sea
And softer moon.

LITTLE FEET

I wait the sound of a quick light tread
Without my door,
The running of two tiny feet
Along the floor;
A moment's silence, and a breathless throb --
And then the quiet turning of the knob.

O, years it seems before the door
Will open wide,
And the impish owner of those feet
Will step inside.
An aeon more -- my thoughts in fear are dressed.
Then -- it is she that I hold to my breast!

The joy of greeting ever makes
It worth the while
To part in sorrow sweet a space --
Then know the smile
And happy face the op'ning door can give;
'Tis for the coming loved one that we live!

I pray that God decree it thus
With you and I,
Tho the absence be for long
Or just a sigh;
That ever thru the years across the floor
Your little feet come softly to my door!

A LIE COMES QUICKER

A lie comes quicker than the truth to tongue
Grown cautious hiding what it seeks to hide;
Yet what can be concealed if breath of lung
Make perjured sounds? The tongue, by having lied,
Says there is something dreading to be known
By one beloved or hated or denied.
What matter then is that the truth be shown,
For silence but agrees that good has died.

And if oppressor -- all is understood
That needs to be for prayers and for tears.
Yet if oppressed -- believe that there is good
Existing stronger than the strongest fears.
So now shall there be silence of a word:
So now shall there be truth unheard or heard.

LOGIC

With Hate nor Love is logic known,
But one is powered from above.
Thus reasoning, I want to be
Illogical with Love.

Charles Gordon Rex

(circa 1941)

Charles Gordon Rex as a baby in 1909 with his parents, Charles George Rex and Ida Maude (Craven) Rex.

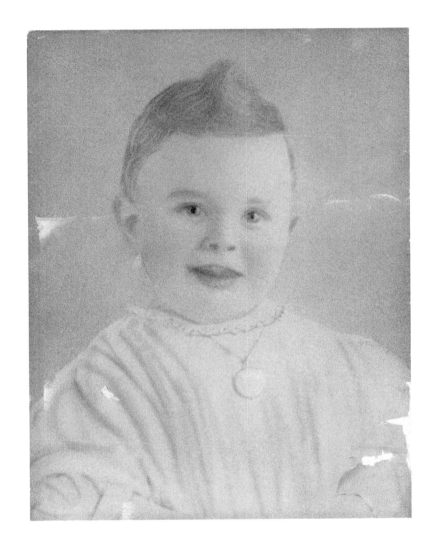

A picture of Charles Gordon Rex as a baby in 1910.

Charles Gordon Rex's mother, Ida Craven Rex (1876 – 1964), circa 1941.

Charles Gordon Rex's father, Charles George Rex (1858 – 1939), at 66 years of age. The elder Charles was a carpenter in Springfield who worked on the construction of some of Springfield's largest buildings.

Charles Gordon Rex circa 1919 strapped in a special sled, probably built by his father to accommodate his paralysis.

Charles Gordon Rex circa 1928 at the start of his singing career.

CHARLES REX
BARITONE

THE art of the miniaturist is the metier of the exquisitely modulated voice of Charles Rex, baritone, now in his sixth year before the public.

Known throughout the East by virtue of his many seasons as a broadcaster with prominent New England stations, as well as his frequent appearances on the concert platform, the sound musicianship displayed by Mr. Rex can perhaps be traced to the fact that he laid his musical foundation when he was six years old, studying piano. Rex, who is an excellent pianist, moving with facility through the works of Bach down to the moderns of today, took up the study of the violin at the age of twelve.

Royal Dadmun was Mr. Rex's vocal mentor for five years, beginning when he was eighteen. More recently he has been working with Mme. Cora Claiborne, prominent voice teacher of Springfield, Mass.

Mr. Rex's many-sided talents include not only the creative spirit which marks his style of singing and recreating the music of the masters, but he is himself a composer of no small ability—having written string quartets, piano pieces and many songs.

PRESS COMMENTS

"There is a poignant quality pervading his interpretations which cannot fail to appeal to even a casual listener."
Springfield Republican

"The voice itself is young and so full of promise that one listens, not only to the sound of it as it is today, but to the hints of what it is bound to be."
Leland Hall, Music Dept., Smith College,
Daily Hampshire Gazette, Northampton

"'On the Seashore of Endless Worlds', a song of great difficulty, Mr. Rex sang in exceedingly effective manner. His top notes were clear and well handled and his entire scale was smooth."
William M. Clark, Springfield Union

"It was not only with volume and unusual beauty of tone that he was able to impress his listeners, but also with a keenness of perception and a successful molding of phrases. The projection of certain emotions and pictures within a narrow scope is the art of a miniaturist, and this art is the distinguishing feature of Mr. Rex's singing."
Benjamin Buxton, Springfield Republican

"If signs do not fail, when the time comes Mr. Rex will take his place in the front rank of singers of our day."
Daily Hampshire Gazette, Northampton

"I count on you as an exponent of whatever value my ideas may have."
Letter from Royal Dadmun

"In addition to being a singer, Mr. Rex has tried his hand at composing, with some success. A short song, entitled, 'Love's Transcendence,' written by him, was included in his final group and stood up bravely with the rest of the program."
Benjamin Buxton, Springfield Republican

"He has a rare sense of musical proportion. In the Prologue to Pagliacci he sang with true dramatic fire, without ever exaggerating. In the old Italian things his singing was beautifully smooth."
Leland Hall, Music Dept., Smith College,
Daily Hampshire Gazette, Northampton

"Mr. Rex sang with excellent German diction and intelligent conception of its varying moods."
Springfield Union

"He has a rich emotional background, and coupled with that a more than satisfactory technic. He is capable of doing worthwhile things."
Springfield Republican

Charles Gordon Rex circa 1945 showing his ability to use crutches in spite of his paralysis and scoliosis. This picture was taken about the time of his junior year at Rollins College. During his vocal career, he would hide his crutches out of the audience's view and support himself on the accompanying piano, only producing them after he had sung.

Charles Gordon Rex circa 1946. He was able to drive using hand controls.

Charles Gordon Rex preparing for Rollins College graduation ceremonies in 1946.

Charles Gordon Rex circa 1948 at about the time of his second marriage while he was on the faculty of Rollins College.

Charles Gordon Rex holding his son, Charles, Jr., shortly after his birth in 1949.

Charles Gordon Rex during the Christmas season of 1949.

Charles Gordon Rex with his 4-month-old son Charles, Jr., at Christmas time in 1949.

Charles Gordon Rex, circa 1954.

Charles Gordon Rex in his darkroom, circa 1949.

Charles Gordon Rex working at his hobby of photography, circa 1949.

A Rex Family Christmas during the holiday season of 1952. Left to right: Charles Gordon Rex, Charles Gordon Rex, Jr., Christopher Davis Rex, and Betty Helen Rex.

Charles Gordon Rex with his three children, Charles, Jr., Christopher, and Cathy, circa 1957.

Charles Gordon Rex in an early electric wheelchair circa 1963. More like a small golf cart, it was heavy and had to be transported in a small trailer.

The tombstone for Charles Gordon Rex. At the top of the stone is engraved the theme from his Violin Sonata. At the bottom is the line "It Is My Soul That Sings" from what was probably his most autobiographical poem, "Listen to My Song," which was read at his funeral.

LOVE

To love means so much more than this:
   A fervent embrace, a stormy kiss,
   A body warm held close in bliss.

   It is self, forgotten, free of mire,
   The end of all uncouth desire;
It is friendship, home, and an open fire!

THE LOVES WE KNEW

Yesterday the loves we knew
Then seemed the only winds that blew.
Today the air is warm and kind;
Tomorrow it may chill us through.

MARCH AND THE MAIDEN

Loud March, wind-shattered,
Tired with the fight,
His garments tattered,
Stands aside for April,
His hair awry.

Blonde April, with timid sighs
Stepping daintily,
Raises tear-wet eyes,
For, seeing his wild look, she knows
He is soon spent, and passes by

Lifting her soft white skirt
Clear of Winter's battle-ground.
Giving her curls a toss and flirt,
She dances off to a green-clad world
Leaving poor, ragged March to die.

MUSING IN AN UNKNOWN TONGUE

I am upon a desert isle
Where old outnumber young,
And all the sparse words uttered
Are in an unknown tongue.

I picked a word up here and there
And saved them up to say
The tiniest of all the thoughts
That filled my head each day.

And when I had a thousand,
I put a few together
And later found that I had made
A comment on the weather.

Of all the words that I had learned,
No solitary one
But simply said the day was dull
Or marked how warm the sun!

MY CHILDREN'S MOTHER

Such time has passed that I can hear her name
And feel no sudden pang of nameless fear:
And I can even hear a person say,
"She married again," as though he said,
"She lies in bed at night with someone else."

I can even see a recent picture
Of her, and, feeling nothing, say nothing,
Except to note she's looking older now,
But no way wiser, nor even kinder.

But ah, at night! At night -- that's different!
She smiles and speaks softly, and my spirit
Softens, and I believe once more the things
That never were true, nor even existed;
That never could exist, as everyone knew --
Except the one who was most deluded.

Yes, when night comes, how imperceptibly
   Her face changes from soft to sardonic,
   And I, humiliated, writhe and sweat --
   So hopeless, worthless, until her silence
   Becomes an unbearable crash of sound
That shatters me to pain and consciousness
So that I can, once more, endure her name,
And feel no sudden pang of nameless fear.

And this, somehow, she knows, and silently
Comes across the years, and, once more smiling
   Softly and gently, so that my spirit,
   Waiting in the wings to raise the curtain,
Does so, then slowly walks to center-stage.

MY FINEST THOUGHTS

I call, but my finest thoughts come not out of their sanctum.
Yet when I am silent, they quietly open the door
And come to stand by my side. And I welcome them and rejoice
That they have come, for I know not the secret of their hiding places.

(Originally published in *First Things*)

NATURE'S PLAN

Would any tears of man deter the sun?
Or all his sorrows cloud the riotous spring?
Could any plan of nature once begun
Be changed or altered for a simple thing
As frightened bird that halts its fluttering
To cock its head and dart despairing eyes
Toward where a hawk is cruelly following,
And show its fear of death in frantic cries?

Too mighty is the universe to call
Such happenings as life destroyed for meat
A tragedy; it matters not at all
That souls are bartered for enough to eat.
Thus reasoning, why should we think our prayers
Important in a cosmic God's affairs?

NO PLACE FOR ME

This is no place for me today, I thought,
Too much joy -- too much laughter
For one dedicated the day before
To a life of sorrow -- and more after.

With tear-filled eyes, I turned and ran,
Tripped when I would get away --
Tripped, and fell gratefully into your arms --
Glad of reprieve -- and to forswear yesterday.

NO TALKING NOW

No talking how; I'm tired of all I said.
Of all I meant, and all I did not mean,
And all I did not say. Now let us clean
The foils on which we all too often bled
And put them by the wall to rust instead;
We shall not need them more, so let them lean,
And throw away the stone that kept them keen.
This is the truce, -- with neither of us dead;

And this, I think, is yet the better part:
We did not die, and so at last we knew
What thing it was that stung us to the heart;
What thing that each believed the other threw.
The pain we felt was more than that of dart,
But does that matter now to me or you?

NOVEMBER

Plunge your hands in fresh-piled leaves;
Colored leaves all crisp and dry,
Fling them in a high cascade
Up toward the blue-frost sky.

Deeply breathe the Autumn wind,
Smell the pungent smoke of Fall,
Watch the thrifty, flicking squirrel,
Hear a thousand voices call.

Feel the brown and hard-packed earth
Thudding underneath your tread,
Mark the echo of a twig
Snapping where a deer has fled.

Evening's red and morning's mist,
Nut-burrs burst within the wood,
Cat-tails wave their ragged velvet
Where the spindly cranes have stood.

OF BEAUTY

Of beauty one is never sure to know
All parts; or even what the cause may be
That sets it halo-wise upon a tree;
Or seeing it dissolve, one may not show
In demonstration how that thus and so
Contrived to bring its end; no chemistry
Concocted yet has set its secrets free
That man at will can make it fade or grow

It may unbidden, root itself in slime;
Or ice upon a mountain top a span
Austere and white; or, for the merest breath,
Envelope all that still exists in time.
Yet beauty's fate is one with that of man,
If beauty cannot live beyond his death.

OF PASSION

Delicate, oh, how delicate
Is the faint stirring
Of passion
In the heart of youth.
It is the whirring
Of tiny wings
In a soft white breast.

Thunderous, oh, how thunderous
Is the throbbing heat
Of passion
In the heart of man.
It is the wild beat
Of echoing drums
In a flame-red morning.

Cheerless, oh, how cheerless
Is the last fluttering
Of passion
In the heart of age.
It is the sputtering
Of a spent flame
That dies in the night.

OH, COME, MY LOVE

Oh, come, my love and spend a day with me
Where we can be apart from all the world;
There we shall lie beneath a shady tree
And watch the lazy mists of heaven, unfurled
Upon a field of blue which hours agone
Will deepen, deepen almost unto black,
And stars will nestle close and wait the dawn
As you shall wait, the earth beneath your back.

The stars will be for you, your eyes for me
To look deep into worlds that must remain
Unknown to both of us. Yet what we see
Will stir us both and bring, unbearably,
The paralyzing spasms of delight
Which end our day, and hold us through the night.

AN OLD GARDEN IN WINTER

Beneath the tumbling monuments of old trees
Lie the dead of marigolds, phlox, and asters.

The first chill wind had bowed their heads;
The herald snow now whispers over their crumbling brownness.

A host of flowers have lived and died here,
A recurrent resurrection. Year by year
Yellow banners and purple have fluttered in a kinder breeze
Than now. More and more askew, the weather-scarred trees
Have had their inscriptions effaced and recarved
By hammers of wind and chisels of ice. To the starved
Birds, for a century have come the legacies of flowers.
Sadness, without tears, is theirs who remember the hours
Of gentle gaiety, cultured pageantry that now has flown.
Here, a hundred years of flowers have blown.

ON MOVING TO FLORIDA

These woods are not the kind of woods I know;
The moss-hung pines and palm trees standing here
Are alien to my eyes, as, hot and slow,
They stir before a sullen wind. I fear
That should I live among them year for year
And find deep-hidden flowers as they show
Themselves, uncovered by the wind, no tear,
Because of sudden loveliness, would flow.

Instead, such beauty, riotously nude,
And innocent, unraped by sleet and snow,
Would find me soon forgetting I intrude,
As I was taught to think in woods I know
Where flowers bright as these are never viewed;
Or if they are, no one will tell you so.

ON SEEING A WHITE MOTH IN TIMES SQUARE

Frail alien, shattering
Your white wings
In the rumble and clattering
Of a thousand things
That grind and roar;
Where whistling, shrill,
Stands the law opening the door
Of traffic; cars mill
And scream with pain
Until the law
Closes it again.
Clamor! And here are you in its claw
With frightened dust,
Minute, infinitesimal,
Falling from pulsing wings. Must
Your death be slow -- gradual?

Could not some hand other than this,
With its thousand fingers of din and smoke,
Toss the chill kiss
Of Death? You broke
The persistent rush of sound
With your calm white,
And on the ground
Settles the dust of your flight.
Through the teeming street
There bloom at night
A million flowers to greet
The dark: glass and all alight.
O White Moth! Why did you not stay in some
Silent wood where rise pied,
Delicate flowers? Pale Moth, why did you come
Here, -- here! Where beauty has long since died?

ON READING A BORROWED BOOK

We talked and smiled, and brightly from our lips
    Fell tiny talk and absent-minded quips;
    We ever were polite as we were taught
    But wondered what the other truly thought.

    Yet now today I need no further look;
    I found your heart encompassed by a book:
Your fears and hopes revealed by those long dead,
    Their dreams re-fancied often as you read.

Beside each phrase that matched the silent truth
    That in us all has everlasting youth,
    Your marks were clear and audible as well.
    They told me all your lips would never tell.

    I know you love the joy of wind and rain,
And welcome snow but yearn for Spring again,
    Or love a friend and enemies forgive,
And have a creed by which you strive to live.

The truth that's sought may not be where we look,
    For you were in the pages of a book.
Thus seeking self, to know my heart's own light,
    Perhaps it shines within the things I write.

OUR LITTLE MINDS

Our little minds are much too small
To grasp the greatness of it all.
Some men puff with ego's bloat
And they but on the surface float.
Thirst may cause men to aspire
To drink the wine of things entire,
But when we know how small we are
We've found the way to touch a star!

OUR THOUGHTS

We never say our thoughts,
For fear of reprimand;
We laugh them with the others,
And toss them out of hand.

But night is most persistent.
Retrieves them one by one,
And bids us think of them alone,
Concealed from sun.

PARADOX

When I felt that there was nothing more to fear,
    A thousand fears arose before my eyes.
When I thought that I at last had found a truth,
    I was conscious of a multitude of lies.

    I sat me down and said, "I am content,"
And knew that there was much to be desired;
    I trained myself in arts to bring me fame,
And now that I am fit, I've grown too tired.

And when we die, not one can surely say,
    "There he lies beneath this grassy mound."
    I draw a steady bow across the strings,
And yet I know not whither goes the sound.

A PARK

There are pigeons and squirrels in the park;
The pigeons flutter about an old man.
Squirrels become statues at his feet for neglect;
Or wind-borne gray fluff for a nut --
The pigeons and squirrels in the park....
And an old man in whom there is wisdom.

PERSPECTIVE

How can we speak of love the while
That war is on the way?
Yet doves are cooing in the cote
While buzzards seek their prey.

How can we sing of beauty when
Dissolutions frown?
Yet morning birds have sung at dawn
O'er many a smould'ring town.

What can there be of music
Save the sounds of hostile treads?
Yet marigolds are rampant now
And toss their golden heads.

I will not hear, I will not see
A momentary strife
That speaks of death: I only know
The things that speak of life.

For love is life and hate is death,
And this is plain to see:
Our hands shall fashion death of hate,
And that's enough for me.

THE POET WOOS IN ANCIENT STYLE

At thy bestowing commendation
On my humble songs to thee,
I am filled with trepidation
Lest you think not, too, of me.

Good, thou call'st my verse, and tender;
Oft I've seen thy gaze go far.
But if thy love they not engender,
What care I how good they are?

From the heav'ns I pluck them, singing,
Lay them at thy tiny feet;
Then thy thoughts oft go swinging,
Nor yet return to love complete.

If thou wilt never out from heaven
Pluck a song and me-ward sing,
Then bread I am that hath no leaven,
An harp that's mute on ev'ry string!

If thou wilt never hear my pleading,
Never turn thine eyes on me,
My heart will broken be and bleeding,
Yet still will hold a song for thee!

Fair thou art, thou Queen of Grace,
But if, like jewels from out thy throat,
Fond words of love thy praise replace –
More fair thou art then e'er I wrote!

POTENTIALITY

Aftermath of seed is present tree,
Its manifest potentiality.
Analysis of seed declares it bound,
Its single freedom happenstance of ground.

PRESENCE

Some day when you are sitting quietly,
Concerned with nothing else but what is there
Around you in the room that you can see,
Some vague unrest will seize you in your chair,
And lift you up, and follow as you walk,
And see you scowling trying to recall
What things we said when there was time for talk;
What other things we never said at all.

No chair will tell you where it was I sat
And read your thoughts aloud as from a book;
No object left as tangible as that,
And you will not remember what you took.
For what you have of me, expect at most
That I shall plague you like an unseen ghost.

PRISONER

So now a thousand days have paused and passed,
And left the signs of thousands yet to be:
An army, representing you, amassed
To storm the troubled battlements of me.
And each is led by some degree of you,
First, one by one, and then complete, entire,
Till I, besieged and pierced through and through,
Await with lowered head the final fire.

Yet even while my abject eyes drop low,
And seek the earth, unwilled to show defeat,
Though winning does not suit me, well I know
Surrendering need not be so complete.
For though I could have won, let it be said,
I chose to be your prisoner instead.

PROFUNDITY

Profundity is not your coat-of-arms,
Nor wisdom your escutcheon,
Your armor is not faith,
Nor your sword truth.

For were they, no gallant knight
That ever lived need have.
And even Christ might have saved
The humility of victory and defeat,
The one, two thousand years ago,
The other, just today.

QUEST

The silver music of dawn,
Calm as slumber,
I have heard times without number,--
Then it was gone.

Where does all music go?
That of quiet hills,
Of muted rills,
Or the echo of sounds through falling snow?

The singing heart of one
Now silent, I would hear again--
But living song, not as the wind across the fen
Bringing faint perfume of flowers nodding in the sun.

I knew the beauty of our years
Would pass and I could not speak,
Nor stay their dying cadence. Now I seek
But the echo of their song through falling tears.

RESPITE

How kind that winter did not come this year
To wound the trees and grass with frosty knife,
And sever bird-song from the listening ear,
Killing here, or there suspending life;
Yet everywhere denuding to the cold
The timid and the hardier of hide,
And making no concession to the old,
But sealing earth from them when they have died.

How kind it was that winter did not come,
But let the earth choose if it should die or sleep,
And let us listen to the vibrant hum
Of insects in the flowers we chose to keep.
Two years is rather more than it could bear;
Perhaps it came -- perhaps we were not there.

THE RED-BREASTED GROSBEAK

In the quiet jungle thicket
At evening rose a summer cricket
With oft-repeated note;
Above him in my maple tree
I heard and watched quite breathtakingly
The lovely ruby-throat.

Entranced I stood and watched him long
And revelled in his swelling song
Of strange and pure desire.
Then wild within me thrilling came
An unsuspected, answering flame,
Vying with his throat of fire.

He vanished from the trembling tree
And gently swayed the bough where he
His clear full song had made.
Then in the quiet, jungle thicket
I heard once more the plaintive cricket
Beneath the maple shade.

I waited long before I heard
This lovely, strange, elusive bird
Of wild and thrilling note;
But now more beautiful to me
Shall stand my sturdy maple tree
Since came the ruby-throat!

THE ROSE IN THE BOOK

I cogitated long about this rose
Pressed thin by the pages of a book;
The bright color is gone from its once lovely petals,
But about it there is an aura of memories.

What there is to remember, I do not know --
I cannot truly call to life the past;
It may be that a lover silently told of his love
As he proffered this symbol ancient as mankind.

Then, too, in freedom from the bonds of school,
Dressed in white, straight and tall,
Perhaps you wore it clasped to your slim waist,
And happily walked your way across the stage.

And still another memory arises from this rose,
Seen, like the others only in imagination --
Coquetishly you wear it in your hair
Just for him who brightens your eyes;

For him who makes the pulse quicken in your throat;
Him for whom you laugh in breathless fashion,
Flinging back your head in innocent abandon,
Giving yourself with your eyes and lips and heart.

I do not know if I have fathomed the past.
Perhaps I shall never know, but I am glad,
For in this rose there is music that will play on
Long after the last petal has crumbled into dust.

SEA MOODS

Blue in its cajoling,
Yellow in its anger;
Ever luring,
Ever scowling,
Murmuring softly,
Roaring madly,
Smiling gently
With pregnant silence.

THE SEA

The sea calls and men go running down to the water's edge.
They stand looking out over the mystery of waters.
Waves boisterously break upon the shore and dance away
With beckoning hands.

The sea calls and men go running down to the water's edge.
They fashion frail boats and journey out searchingly,
Wide-eyed, like children.

The sea calls and men go running down to the water's edge.
They stand looking out over the mystery of waters.
They fashion frail boats and journey out searchingly.
After long silences they return,
And wisdom is hard in their eyes.

THE SEASONS FLUTTER

The seasons flutter
About me like leaves
Shaken from a tree
By winds of autumn.
Faster they are whirled
To the ground,
So fast now
That I cannot watch
Their grace,
Nor see their lovely
Patterns.
Soon it may be
The tree will trace
A slim, dark pattern itself
Against the sky,
And I will sink to rest
Among the bright days
That I have lived.

THE SEEKER

Here I am, half-way to dawn;
Is the journey long?
May I rest? Is what is gone
Quite enough for song?

You, somewhere,-- do you seek the sun?
Is it dark for you?
Do you sleep? Have you begun
Thinking eyes are through

Closing ever? Does your mind
Leap ahead to light?
Do you strain your eyes to find
Thin, gray streaks? Will night

End for you as it began?
You are there, and I
Still seek answers no one can
Tell this side of sky.

You there, do you see the sun?
Will the day suffice?
Here, outside of Eden, none
Guess at Paradise.

SILENCE

No man is silent who has that to give
Which may bring light or joy to them who hear,
Unless it be that while he yet may live,
They cannot know his words and even fear
The way his words may point. Thus tacitly,
And knowing well that sound cannot prevail,
He goes unspeaking to the gallows tree,
That silence may effect where words may fail.

And that is one; another, he who grieves;
But two there are, and all the rest for shame
Take refuge in the reticence of thieves,
And call each other by a common name.
Not sad, but mute? Nor Christ at Pilate's bar?
Your silence then shall tell me who you are.

THE SNOW DANCES

The snow dances ahead of the wind,
Tauntingly, for never may it stay behind.
The wind howls in rage and blows itself out
While the snow settles and gracefully dies,
Knowing that it shall laugh again, --
Reincarnate.

SOLITARY

Deadlier than Death is solitary to stand
In the crowded market place
Speaking a tongue unknown.
What terror to be imprisoned
Behind eyes wherein no one looks
To discover who quakes and quivers there,
Crying out for help
With the great voice of Silence.

SOMETIME, PERHAPS NOT VERY FAR AWAY

Sometime, perhaps not very far away,
I shall make answer where before was none;
And you will listen gravely while I say
What I have never said to anyone
Except where it was true as words are true!
I did not know (as well as now I know)
In those past years before there was a you,
That more than talk must be to make it so.

Sometime, I say, you will have heard it all:
How, in the shadow of three mossy trees,
Where just today I heard the bluejays call,
I asked, I know not whom, for such as these:
Three wishes (though but two of us is found)
That someday (counting us) may just go round!

SONG OF THE HARVEST

A bright blue banner is unfurled: the sky!
A blast from a golden trump is hurled on high!
Over the hills there comes a shining knight,
Majestic, noble, and scattering before him – Light!

It echoes in the vale like a kingly horn
And turns to yellow the stalks of waving corn;
It shatters itself to colors on tree and vine
And fills the air with the tang of new-made wine.

Gray-blue rocks and meadow-red and dun:
The spectrum of the golden-armored sun!
Fleecy manners! Flags of blue and gold;
The bright blade of the river, steely cold.

Onward ride! The harvest now is won!
From battle rides the golden-armored sun
Down the royal road of Autumn Days –
A multitude of voices sing his praise!

SOUNDS

Some sounds we wait to hear, as when at night
   We cannot sleep, or do not want to sleep
     Until the birds are cognizant of light,
       And tree and bush and rock no longer keep
        Their presence hidden, but begin to show
       Themselves to be as real as when they stood
     The night before and saw the sunlight go,
  And darkness silenced birds and hid the wood.

    Yet other sounds, not even being heard,
     Tell what has died and what has only slept,
      And show what song was never that of bird,
      And what was lost that never could be kept.
       No need to wait for these, nor to deny
That had we stayed, we should have said goodbye.

SPRING THAW

Along the eaves
The brittle icicles drip.
The water-drops never once
Fly wide their goal.

The liquid spheres
Fall free in the sunlit air
And bore down deep in the snow
A small round hole.

A STRAY THOUGHT

Did you ever pause to think before
That on this swiftly moving planet
The slightest relative wind could blow
Us off like dust from polished granite?

STRENGTH

The rocks cling to the Mother Mountain,
 The trees embrace the fruitful Earth;
And our souls should ever be as these --
Gathering strength, One from the Other.

SUNRISE

I waited at dawn for the rising sun,
But he drew a veil of clouds before his face;
His brightness was too great for one
Who has long waited in darkness.

A TELLER OF TALES

He stood before me, bright of face,
And told the weirdest tales:
How in a plane he'd soared through space,
And how he'd harpooned whales.

How far off in a southern spot
Some cannibals he'd met;
He'd helped them hang a big iron pot
And get the table set.

But then he'd had to run away
And take the longest swim,
Not 'cause he wasn't asked to stay,
But they'd have dined on him!

I told him I was not amused,
That when a table's set,
He shouldn't leave until excused,
It wasn't etiquette.

To which he gravely took the stand
    That it was not polite
To give a dinner party and
    Eat all the guests in sight!

I quite agreed and told him so,
    Admitting my mistake,
Suggesting that we both should go
    And eat a piece of cake.

He held me back and bade me stay
    And told me without jest
An ogre stood within the way
    To guard the treasure chest.

And if we did not use great care
    We surely would be caught.
It called for courage, do and dare
    To gain the goal we sought.

So we got down and slowly crept
Along the dark hall floor
Toward where all the cake was kept
Beyond the kitchen door.

My hand had barely reached the knob,
When on our startled ears
There fell a choking sort of sob
That filled our hearts with fears.

We quickly turned and down we sat
And gazed up in despair.
You know what we were looking at --
The ogre standing there!

Its face was red, its eyes aflame,
It seemed to be in pain,
And as we huddled close there came
The sobbing noise again.
Of course, I was the first to break
The awe and fearful spell,
"We thought we'd have a piece of cake --"
The ogre gave a yell:

Her laughter was restrained no more,
We added to the noise.
She scooped my comrade from the floor
And said, "Two little boys!"

Of course, denials loud I cried,
And quickly up I stood.
I tried to act as dignified
As fathers really should.

I brushed my clothes, pulled down my vest,
Then straightened up my tie;
I placed my hand upon my breast
And looked her in the eye.

But 'twas no use, so I gave o'er --
My dignity's a fake --
We three went through the kitchen door
And had our piece of cake.

THAT YOU MAY NOT KNOW

How can I say it that you may not know?
Disguise the meaning so it will not show?
I have re-worded it a hundred times
And set it by. Not even in my rhymes
Could it be made unreadable, abstruse,
And of these both, God knows, I have made use
To keep what I have wanted to inside.
And just so long as there is space to hide
A thing, why not protect it while you can?
Perhaps in dark or half-dark space, the span
Of what's alive may stand and even grow,
Where killing it would be to let it show.

THERE ARE DAYS

There are days when the world
Is a terrible place:
When woods are untidy
And the sky's a disgrace.

There are other days, though,
When the sky is swept clean
And the meadows and forests
Are models of green.

But sometimes an hour
Is all the day needs
To transform a garden
From flowers to weeds.

It truly is strange
How such things can be,
But it's true. I have seen it,
And I know what I see.

THERE IS A CHURCH

There is a church across the way
That needles to the sky,
And I can never think of it,
Nor even pass it by,

Nor even hear its weekly bells,
Nor watch the stragglers-in
Without an unexplained desire
With perfect height to win

That I could look complacent down,
And -- this is very odd --
Relate archaic and current sin
As they appear to God!

THERE WAS A TIME

There was a time,
When I was young,
That the moon hung
In halted climb,
And stars were hung
For her and me.

Another time,
When years went by,
The moon, less shy,
Did steady climb
To stars so high,
We could not see.

And after this,
Another Spring
Arrived to bring
A sweeter kiss--
A stronger wing
With which to fly.

And so they came,
Each taper lit,
To each its bit
Of damp and flame;
To pause or flit
Across the sky.

Let this be so --
A moon to rise,
Dark-passioned eyes
For me to know,
Then sweep the skies
All new and clean.

And after this,
Another day,
Another May,
A sweeter kiss;
A night all gay
With starry sheen.

THERE WERE THOSE YEARS

There were those years when the sweet Spring rain
　　Made the scent of lilacs exquisite pain,
And we wept or dreamed, and our breast grew tight
　　With the beauty and loveliness of the night.

"There was a time -- remember?" we said;
　　"There was a time that now lies dead,
When life was love and the scent flowers,
　　And love was Spring, and Spring was ours."

I know we believed and thought we knew;
　　But dreams are true if aught be true;
And if aught be true, then time has no grave
And returns to the dreamer the dreams he gave.

See! Now we stand in the path of the moon
　　Where the lilies shine and the roses swoon.
Can you see who walks through the garden there --
　　In silence and Spring and the lilac air?

THE THINGS IN HAND

Think about the things in hand,
Not of those for which you've planned,
For the future, come what will,
Can't improve the present. Still
The yearning for tomorrow
Drains today of joy or sorrow!

THIS STRANGE CURRENT

Like a milk-weed seed blown by the wind
I ride on this strange current,
And I know not when I shall rise and fall
Or which turn I shall make --
But I am glad.

THIS TINY LAKE

This tiny lake with pines about its edge,
This liquid disc, has sliced along their base
And passed beneath to cut them like a wedge,
Till now they stand upon its polished face
Assuming postures they had not before,
And each becomes more conversant with each
And loses its identity with shore,
Its roots submerged beneath the flooded beach.
The lake has widened now and is aligned
With sky where earth was welded once to sky,
But earth is gone, and blue with blue defined,
And clouds in both are problems for the eye
Until across the lake a ripple spreads
And laughs that pines should stand upon their heads!

THOSE WHO PASS BY

Within my life come they,--
Fling wide the door.
They walk with me a little way
And are no more.

They come without a sound --
Each one a friend.
I know not whither they are bound,
Nor to what end.

Is there some place for me
Where I must go --
Some goal, the which I cannot see,
Except they show?

Do they, at some command,
Come one by one,
To then shake off my clinging hand
When they be done?

I've found not even they
Their mission know;
They cannot hear my cries to stay
When they must go.

They come so bright -- then dim;
Each one a friend,
Unwittingly a guide for Him
Who marks the end.

THIS VERY MOMENT

Here, now, this very moment, let there be
A silence great enough for me to hear
Your voice; a silence that will bring it clear,
Distinct, and saying what it is that we
Have yet to tell each other; what we fear
To make too plain. And since you cannot see
That I am listening, hand cupped to ear,
Then say it to the wind, and so, to me.

And I will know whatever you may say
As true, and know it better than I knew
Your muteness when you were not miles away
Along an arc of earth; the merest breath
Of distance really, yet as great as death,
If parting us is all that death could do.

THOUGHT FOR THOUGHT

If nothing else had power so to do,
That I have weighed my thought would clearly show
How far it is I stand away from you,
And where it is you walk, and where I go,
And where it is I was and you not so;
And why I balanced thought for thought and knew
That after knowing, you would have to know
As well, as best you could, or wanted to.

For though a bird might think as well as I,
How could he then adjust his flight with care
And wing precisely parallel with sky
If he were drunk with sun and summer air?
No more can you, nor do you want to yet;
And though I can, I hope I shall forget.

THOUGHTS

We cannot shape our thoughts in just the way
A sculptor might transform the rigid stone
Or mold the pliant nonresisting clay.
However well the method may be known,
No mental chisel ever can fulfill
The task of cutting lines where they should fall,
Nor carve the patterns chosen by the will
For thoughts that in themselves are all in all.

We try to bend them into what we know,
Or think we know, or what we try to say;
And yet whatever force the will may show,
Belief goes on its own determined way.
We plan the figure, chisel well each part,
Yet form forever what is in the heart.

THE THRUSH'S SONG

Green lie the hills on every side,
A restless sea where love doth hide,
And thrush sets forth at eventide
    His love-filled lay.

The hills hang still and quiet where
The thrush sings on of hope, despair;
His breeze-borne song just roughs their hair
    And soars away.

(According to an added note on the page on which the poem is hand-written in pencil, now faded with age, this was the author's first poem, written at the age of 19 in 1928.)

'TIS EVENING

'Tis evening, and I feel your presence near me.
Never do you speak because the years are great,
And you can't hear me.
If only now the years could slip away, and I could feel
The living warmth of yesterday, beloved.
But still your tenderness and love are with me now,
As they were long ago
When we were young.

TO DIE

To die beautifully is the mark
Of a brave soul.
To have no conscious fear of the dark,
Or of a dismal, damp hole
In the ground, but only anticipation
Of joyous things to come,
Is a gift bestowed on few,
If some.

I know I shall not die
In a quiet dreaming;
It will not be the giving up of a gentle sigh,
But more protestingly. In fact,--screaming.
I am very certain it will be rough
On everyone when I set out for the sod.
I shall not even be calm enough
Coward to snivel; but relatives, doctor, and God
Will know
I go.

Yet why I should be afraid of oblivion, Heaven, or Hell,
I have no notion.
It is just that to die -- well --
I do everything with emotion!

TO MY WIFE

My songs I scatter hither, hence;
Small of worth and eloquence,
Goalless as a madman's steering,
Written for a moment's hearing.

Love has been a frequent theme,
Swift and changing as a dream.
Seasons, too, have had their place,
As well as every female grace.

Inspirations have been mine,
From ancient hills to new-pressed wine.
I've watched the world and made my choice,
Struck the chord and raised my voice.

And then, one day, through jaded sight,
I saw the world and I were trite;
The songs the Muse of poets bore
Were sung ten thousand times before!

If this were true, my songs were dead,
(As countless people all have said!)
My Muse a dolt with clumping tread;
Different guises -- always bread.

'Twas strange, indeed, this being so,
That I, today, should come to know
A song for which no harp was strung,
An air that never had been sung.

And she that brought the virgin song
Has been here with me all along;
And though my sight is keen, I swear,
The sheen I saw not of her hair!

Nor knew her lovely eyes did shine
Though often they looked into mine.
And look you at her red, curved lips,
Her dainty hands and fingertips.

Because of my complaining bleat
I never knew her voice was sweet;
Nor marked the courage that she gave
To me, who is not half so brave.

O, never need I fear to write
A verse, a song that will be trite;
That fact, no more, shall me deter --
I am the first to write of her!

TO GROW IN GRACE

And if I seek to grow in grace,
Held steadfast by the Master's face,
Nor heed the things that disappear,
Of Truth, perhaps, I'll find a trace.

TO SIT IN JUDGMENT

To sit in judgment --
Deem profligate, unworthy,
Heretical an alien act
New done, --
Is not for me.

Were I time,
With patience to mark the end
Of present sinners
And judge the wrong
Or right of them,
I doubt that I should wait
To see.

TODAY I LIVE

Today I live and know the will
Of destiny, but cannot fill
My life with what tomorrow brings;
Tomorrow is tomorrow still.

TOIL

Oh, noble toil, that keeps the mind from thought
And helps assuage the pain that sorrow wrought.
And with the swelling muscles, taut with strain,
    Comes the gradual numbing of the brain.
      Oh, to work until the body tires,
And, sweating, quenches all impassioned fires;
    Work and sweat until the calloused hands
      Are as the soul that never understands,
    Are as the soul that cannot see the right --
And then to sleep, at last, with endless night.

TOO MANY

There are too many silences
Uncommon hard to bear,
As when a pleasant voice is stilled
By miles of intervening air.

Too many sights and sounds are near
That can't be stored in ears and eyes
To keep the famished senses from
The dearth that in the future lies.

Too often do accustomed things
Breed merely an apparent hate;
They are transformed to loveliness
The instant it becomes too late.

TRANSITION

I
FALLOW

How then to sing　　　　　　In a far place
When the song's laughed down?　　There'll be song again
How shall the eyes raise　　　　Grateful to distant
To the cold frown?　　　　　　And bitter men.

II
TRANSPLANTATION

There's a gull on the lake　　　And there's sun enough
Away from the sea;　　　　　　And a gentle swell
And there's water enough　　　And we've strength enough here
For him and me　　　　　　　To weather it well.

III
GROWTH

Green leaves push green leaves free and clear
And young blossoms and ripe fruit are together here.
There is no decay, no brilliant, colored rot;
Here life is and endures, and death is not.

THE TREE

I chopped it down today,
The tree I had silently battled and hated now
For years; the tree that would have its way
From the moment I planted it. Each bough
Was predestined from a twig to shut out more light,
More sun, more lake, and more of sky.
And this was it. Now the tree is down, and I
Have back all that it hid, all that for years could not be seen
From here: the sky, the lake, and, sometimes, one cloud like a pearl…
But hornets and wasps have for hours bumped the screen:
They have known Armageddon – they, and one small squirrel.

TRIVIALITIES

"I used to do things like that," he said;
    "Now I see no sense at all."
He meant frivolous things, of course,
For sorrow hemmed him like a wall.

TRUTH

A lie comes quicker than the truth to tongue
Grown cautious hiding what it seeks to hide;
Yet what can be concealed if breath of lung
Make perjured sounds? The tongue, by having lied,
Says there is something dreading to be known
By one beloved or hated or denied.
What matters then is that the truth be shown,
For silence but agrees that good has died.

And if oppressor -- all is understood
That needs to be for prayers and for tears.
Yet if oppressed -- believe that there is good
Existing stronger than the strongest fears.
So now shall there be silence or a word;
So now shall there be truth unheard or heard.

VOWS

The promise that from out your lips was given
Must be redeemed and ever be renewed;
For never should such tender vows be riven,
But with eternity should be imbued.

Your lips have pledged themselves to such desires
That, having pledged, shall give in warmth devout,
Even though their touch shall kindle fires,
That never words nor kisses can put out!

WARNING

Could you but with my eyes to see,
Then 'twere no longer you but me.
Yet do I know that this be well,
For we are one in heaven or hell.

My words are sweet? Then say them, too,
As coming not from me, but you!
Take what you will of good to claim,
Or bad, but share the praise or blame.

The best of me, these words of mine,
I the vintner, they the wine.
Then drink them deeply from the cup;
I filled it, now I lift it up.

Your lips the wine shall meet, and there
Be close as buds and summer air.
And if you drink, like Spring and sun,
We are no longer two, but one.

WAVES

They stood at the water's edge; he
Held his mother's hand
And for the first time saw the sea.
His small feet danced on the sand
As each wave broke on the shore,
And his shrill voice called out joyously,
"Please, ocean, do that some more!"

Presently, the tide being on the flow,
A huge wave glided forward like a moving wall
And crashed upon the beach; then, impotent,
It slid along the sand and reached his toe.
He jumped and squealed with laughter, "How high I went!"
I jumped over the biggest one of all!"

WE COME WITHOUT A BY-YOUR-LEAVE

We come without a by-your-leave;
We go the very same.
We don't know what it was we were,
Nor why it is we came.

We only know that we invest
A tidy sum in life,
Get tiny dividends of peace
For large amounts of strife.

WHAT IS PAST

Knowing then that nothing now will last,
Why need we, friends, from joy or sorrow fast?
When both are done and in the furnace cast,
We will not laugh or cry with what is past.

WHAT LURKS BEHIND YOUR EYES

How well I know what lurks behind your eyes:
How sure I am that you make antonyms
Of secret thoughts; and yet whatever guise
They may acquire, whatever dress the whims
And bright deceptions of your tongue may choose
To clothe them in before you let them run,
You may not call me fool, nor may you bruise
My heart, nor mock my pride and think me one.

Too versed I am in all placating ways --
The reassuring hand; the head thrown high
To laugh a grievance down; the steady gaze
Of fine deceivers soothing with a lie --
To let you think me duped; though what I see
May well be just your eyes reflecting me.

WHAT THINGS SHE LOVED

What things she loved were never made to love:
    Two silver vases, angular and tall;
    A teakwood box; an etching hung above
    An antique table placed against the wall;
    A china closet, oak, and very old,
    Yet joined so tightly dust could never pass
    Within to gray the china, banded gold,
    In tranquil piles behind the bellied glass.

These could she love, and fearing no demands
That they might make of her, would often trace
Their contours with her cool caressing hands
    As lovers do a well-beloved face.
And loving them, she had no need for fright,
But slept untouched and undisturbed at night.

WHAT YOU HAVE TO GIVE

If what you have to give and what I ask
Are so unlike that, unrestricted, would
Destroy whatever there might be of good
Between us; if the end of any task
Were different from that desired, to bask
In sun the flower would aspire in vain,
For seeking light would bring deluging rain
Poured lavishly from sky's too eager flask.

No mated bird would then achieve its nest,
No seed its soil, and work that asked for bread
Would no more get it than would dog his bone,
And no man would attain his body's rest.
If such be so, far better were I dead
Than ask a fish of you and get a stone!

WHEN RED LEAVES FALL

In autumn when the red leaves fall,
  So lightly on the drowsy ground,
  And bare once more the vine-clad wall;
When flown had ev'ry summer sound;

  Then do I walk in youth once more
  Amid the woods, rememb'ring still
    The very paths I trod before,
The dull grey morn – the autumn chill.

    Ah, love, remember yet with me
  The wild hedgerow with berries hung,
  The blue smoke-mist on shedding tree
And high geese through the heavens strung.

  The frost that lay on coarse grass, bent,
Once knew our treading -- joyous, light;
Once vanished where our footsteps went
  Like shadows on drift-snow at night.

  Now flown has ev'ry summer sound
And bare once more the vine-clad wall.
  So lightly on the drowsy ground
  In autumn shall the red leaves fall.

THE WHIPPOORWILL

I heard in the night a whippoorwill;
His sad, foreboding song
Crept through the dark to still
All other sounds.

The notes luminous within the wood,
Like phosphorescent tears that slowly dropt
From beneath the night's now evil hood,
More closely drawn.

A phantom bird, a dark shadow that sings --
Whose glowing, silver notes make unseen light
In silences where Fear and Death are Kings
Of veiled domains.

WHY SADNESS

You want to know why sadness?
A sleeping in the Fall?
I know: That we more happy hear
The first bird's call.

WIND STORM

The dawn is later than it was before
When wind was gentle wantonness of air,
And not the broad-beamed blasts that push and tear
Like drunken louts insisting at the door
That those inside had better heed their roar
And let them in, or else with speed prepare
To hold the flimsy fort, and have a care
Lest walls and roof depart and leave but floor.

Small matter it would be to such a horde
If dawn arrived or never came at all;
Their vulgar breath would whistle through the cracks
All day and night, and every loosened board
That failed to gain them entrance through the wall
Would make them rage at trees and break their backs.

WORDS

How beautiful are words
That come from lips that love them.
And sounds --
Do they not fly more silvery
When the heart sings with them?

YOU STAND BEFORE ME

You stand before me,
Beautiful – bewildered:
Too aware of life.

You are frightened,
For the choice
Is too great:

There is love --
You reach out eager hands,
Then close them --
Empty.

There are stars,
And your eyes grow dark
With longing and glance away --
Tear-filled.

There is song,
And melody rushes through you;
Your lips tremble --
And are mute.

Do you not see?
There is no choice --
Love is a song, and the stars
Are its dwelling place.

Lift your eyes --
Come, let me show you!
Far off there
Stretches infinity;

It is all yours --
I give it to you,
For it has always been yours
To take.

And there is music --
Flowing, singing,
And soon
You will hear it, too.

My quiet dreaming is done;
Thus, you are not here.
But it may be that you will know
If I say:

"Your hands are not empty --
Nor your lips mute,
For there have been roses --
And a kiss."

A YOUTHFUL THOUGHT

Life, how you beckon one
To come out into the sunlight,
Into the warmth of love and music,
Where mountains laugh at the sky,
And people shout their freedom,
Their voices echoing
Like the sound of a mighty cascade
Whose spray catches the sun
And float away
In many rainbows –
Life, how you beckon one!

Death, how you sober one!
To come out into the sunlight,
Into the warmth of love and music,
Where mountains laugh at the sky,
And people shout their freedom,
Only to see you there,
Dim in the distance, with wide-spread arms,
Ready to catch the light
And cover all
In many shadows –
Death, how you sober one!

ZENITH

No better way to enter?
No better way to leave?
Then life is best at center,
For which the ends must grieve.

Pain is the soul of waiting,
Agony that of death;
Suffering marks the taking
And giving up of breath.

But love is the sun of being;
And zenith for both is best
In point of warmth and seeing
When traveling East to West.

About the Editor

Photo by Chris Lee

Charles Gordon Rex, Jr.

Violinist Charles Rex, former Associate Concertmaster of the New York Philharmonic, was born into a musical family in Winter Park, Florida, where his father was a composer and instructor at Rollins College, and his mother taught piano. He started his violin studies at age four under Alphonse Carlo, professor of violin at Rollins. Following his solo debut with the Florida Symphony at age thirteen, Mr. Rex won the Hinda Honigmann Scholarship Award to the Brevard Music Center in North Carolina and toured as soloist with the BMC Orchestra throughout North and South Carolina.

Mr. Rex was awarded a full scholarship to Florida State University, where he studied with Richard Burgin, former Concertmaster and Associate Conductor of the Boston Symphony. Other teachers included Ruth Posselt and Berl Senofsky. In 1982, Florida State University honored him as a Distinguished Alumnus, and the FSU School of Music presented him with the Ernst von Dohnányi Faculty Citation for Excellence in Performance.

Immediately after graduating *cum laude* from FSU with Bachelor and Master of Music degrees in performance, Mr. Rex joined the Philadelphia Orchestra under Eugene Ormandy where he played for eight years before accepting the position of Associate Concertmaster of the New York Philharmonic under Zubin Mehta and Leonard Bernstein, a post he held for 19 years. In 1988, he toured Egypt and Jordan as soloist with the Princeton Chamber Orchestra under conductor Mark Laycock and was the first American to appear as soloist in the new Cairo Opera House. The PBS documentary about this tour, "Classical Caravans," was honored with an Emmy Award. The Borough of Staten Island of New York City also made March 13 of that year "Charles Rex Day" on the occasion of a special recital he performed there on behalf of the New York Philharmonic. Mr. Rex has also served as interim concertmaster of the London Symphony under Sir Colin Davis for a tour of England. In 1999, he relinquished the position of Associate Concertmaster of the New York Philharmonic due to an increasing demand on his time for solo appearances and recordings.

About the Editor

Photo by Chris Lee

Charles Gordon Rex, Jr.

Violinist Charles Rex, former Associate Concertmaster of the New York Philharmonic, was born into a musical family in Winter Park, Florida, where his father was a composer and instructor at Rollins College, and his mother taught piano. He started his violin studies at age four under Alphonse Carlo, professor of violin at Rollins. Following his solo debut with the Florida Symphony at age thirteen, Mr. Rex won the Hinda Honigmann Scholarship Award to the Brevard Music Center in North Carolina and toured as soloist with the BMC Orchestra throughout North and South Carolina.

Mr. Rex was awarded a full scholarship to Florida State University, where he studied with Richard Burgin, former Concertmaster and Associate Conductor of the Boston Symphony. Other teachers included Ruth Posselt and Berl Senofsky. In 1982, Florida State University honored him as a Distinguished Alumnus, and the FSU School of Music presented him with the Ernst von Dohnányi Faculty Citation for Excellence in Performance.

Immediately after graduating *cum laude* from FSU with Bachelor and Master of Music degrees in performance, Mr. Rex joined the Philadelphia Orchestra under Eugene Ormandy where he played for eight years before accepting the position of Associate Concertmaster of the New York Philharmonic under Zubin Mehta and Leonard Bernstein, a post he held for 19 years. In 1988, he toured Egypt and Jordan as soloist with the Princeton Chamber Orchestra under conductor Mark Laycock and was the first American to appear as soloist in the new Cairo Opera House. The PBS documentary about this tour, "Classical Caravans," was honored with an Emmy Award. The Borough of Staten Island of New York City also made March 13 of that year "Charles Rex Day" on the occasion of a special recital he performed there on behalf of the New York Philharmonic. Mr. Rex has also served as interim concertmaster of the London Symphony under Sir Colin Davis for a tour of England. In 1999, he relinquished the position of Associate Concertmaster of the New York Philharmonic due to an increasing demand on his time for solo appearances and recordings.

Mr. Rex has been soloist with the New York Philharmonic numerous times on ten different concerti including Vivaldi's "Four Seasons" and the violin concerti of Tchaikovsky and Nielsen. His performance of the Hindemith Violin Concerto with the Philharmonic was released on a special fund-raising CD for the NYP's Radiothons. He and his brother Christopher Rex, Principal Cellist of the Atlanta Symphony, gave the world premiere of Stephen Paulus' Concerto for Violin and Cello, a work that the New York Philharmonic commissioned especially for the two brothers for the Philharmonic's 150th anniversary season in conjunction with the Atlanta Symphony. Other significant premieres by Charles Rex include the New York premiere of John Harbison's Violin Concerto and the world premieres of Gunther Schuller's "Concerto Quaternio" with the New York Philharmonic, American composer David Ott's Violin Concerto commissioned by the Reading (PA) Symphony, and American composer Mary Jeanne van Appledorn's "Rhapsody for Violin and Orchestra." Other solo appearances have included performances with the Atlanta Symphony, the Cincinnati Symphony, the Charlotte Symphony, the Tucson Symphony, the Milwaukee Symphony, the Denver Chamber Orchestra, the Charleston and Florida Symphonies, the Manhattan Philharmonic, the Queens Philharmonic, and the Transylvania, Reading, and Northwest Indiana Symphonies. As a teacher, Mr. Rex has given public master classes on three continents.

Charles Rex and his brother, cellist Christopher Rex, are featured as soloists on an Elysium label release of Saint-Saëns " La Muse et le Poète " for violin, cello and orchestra, accompanied by the Bohuslav Martinu Philharmonic of the Czech Republic under Peter Tiboris. Other recordings by Charles Rex include the Copland Piano Quartet for EMI and the world premiere recording for Opus One label of the "Rhapsody for Violin and Orchestra" by Mary Jeanne van Appledorn, accompanied by the Polish National Radio Orchestra under Joel Suben.

Mr. Rex retired from the New York Philharmonic in 2017 and taught for two years as Professor and Chair of Music History at the Holy Apostles College and Seminary where he was presented with an honorary Doctorate of Humane Letters in the spring of 2019.

Praise for Charles Rex, Jr.

"...played the solo part deftly and with a silvery sound."

--- THE NEW YORK TIMES

"...his deep-set eyes resembling those of the legendary Paganini, Rex is a born performer who projected with elegance, beauty and technical élan."

--- THE NEW YORK POST

"His will be a name to remember...(he) had no trouble sending the audience into raptures."

---LOUISVILLE TIMES

"Rex is an articulate player whose left hand is exacting and who commands a full sound...In those rich chords that start the final movement (of the Prokofiev Violin Concerto No. 2), the clarity of his intonation let the violin sing ardently above the surging orchestra support."

--- THE PHILADELPHIA INQUIRER

"...a stunning piece...stunningly realized...stellar standards. Who could ask for more?"

--- THE ATLANTA CONSTITUTION

"Rex plays the (Mendelssohn) concerto with an ease of manner that momentarily hides a deeply romantic interpretation...This is one of the best live performances I have heard of the piece."

--- THE DENVER POST

Made in the USA
Middletown, DE
08 December 2023

43851679R00146